Lord Rothschild and the Barber

The struggle to establish the London Jewish Hospital

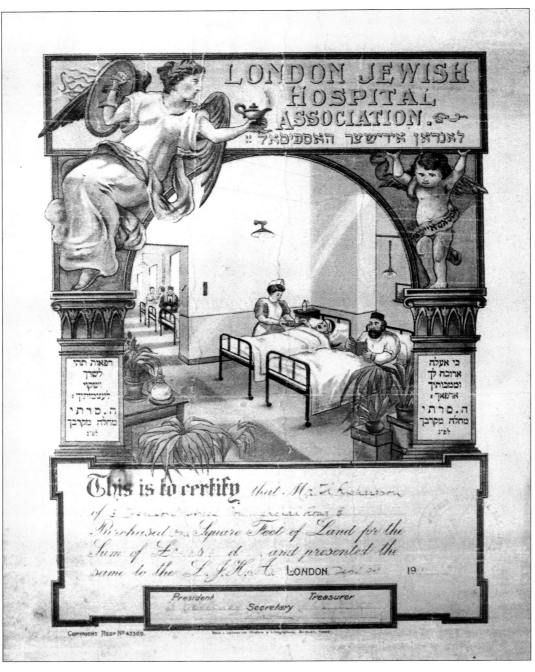

(I) *Certificate issued to Mr Hyman Richardson in 1910 to acknowledge his purchase of one foot of land on the Stepney Green site. It is signed by the Association's Chairman, Isidor Berliner, the Treasurer, Anghel Gaster, and the Secretary, Nathan Jacobowicz.* [*Montague Richardson*]

Lord Rothschild and the Barber

The struggle to establish the London Jewish Hospital

GERRY BLACK

TYMSDER PUBLISHING

First published in Great Britain in 2000 by Tymsder Publishing
PO Box 16039
London NW3 6WL
e-mail tymsder@aol.com

British Library Cataloguing in Publication Data
A catalogue record for this book is available from the British Library

ISBN 0-9531104-3-5

Typesetting and production by The Studio, Exeter

For my wife, Anita

CONTENTS

THE LONDON JEWISH HOSPITAL BEFORE NATIONALISATION

THE LONDON JEWISH HOSPITAL AFTER NATIONALISATION

ACKNOWLEDGEMENTS

During my research for this book, I have made use of the volumes set out in the Select Bibliography, (and many others), and examined archives relating to the London Jewish Hospital; the London Hospital; Mile End Old Town Infirmary; Whitechapel Infirmary; the German Hospital; the Metropolitan Hospital; the Mildmay Mission Hospital; the Jewish Board of Guardians (now Jewish Care); the United Synagogue; the Gaster papers; and the Rothschild archives. I should like to thank the archivists concerned, all of whom were unfailingly helpful, as were the staff of the Newspaper Library at Colindale, the Public Record Office at Kew, London Metropolitan Archives, the Hartley Library at Southampton University, the Jewish Museum Manchester, the Jewish Museum, London and the British Library. The *Jewish Chronicle* and the *Jewish World* were particularly fruitful sources of information.

Many people and organisations have assisted by providing documents, photographs, and suggestions, by responding to my letters, and by sparing time for interviews. I am particularly indebted to Sylvia Ark, Rabbi Y. Y. Abrahams, Bill Bean, Doreen Berger, Rene Bergerman, W. V. Berliner, Rabbi Pesach Black, Stephanie Black, Anita Blumberg, Dr H. Cohen, Alice Collins, John Cooper, Dr A. A. Davis, Judith Devons, John Eversley, Yvette Fehler, Renee Goldsmith, Hugh Goodman Levy, Brian Gordon, the late Ian Gordon, Rhoda Hackman, Lysbeth Hurstbourne, Dr Joseph Jacob, Jim Jarretts, Raymond Kalman, Anne Kershen, Dr Lionel Kopelowitz, Ruth Kugelmann, Suzanne Leigh, Ruby Lewis and the late Cyril Lewis (a grandson of Isidor Berliner), Joy Lyons, Dr Lara Marks, Lottie Newman, the late Israel Prieskel, Anthony Radcliffe, Don Rainger, David Ricardo, Monty Richardson, Enid Rosenberg (granddaughter), Manny Rosenberg, Aumie Shapiro, Rose Shaw, Gerald Smith (grandson), Louis Starr, Hannah Hedwig Striesow, Sylvia Wallis, the Wolfson Foundation.

To them, and to all the others who helped in a myriad number of ways, I give my sincerest thanks.

My greatest debt is to my wife, Anita, to whom this book is dedicated.

The frontispiece is dedicated by Montague (Monty) Richardson as a tribute to his late father Hyman Richardson; a devout Jew, a tailor who was typical of the working class supporters of the movement who were determined to establish a Jewish Hospital in London. It also records Monty's gratitude to the late Mr Israel Prieskel and the staff at the Hospital for the treatment and care he received in 1959 when he was suffering a life-threatening illness.

LIST OF ILLUSTRATIONS

They had to work and labour and strive and contrive for pennies and halfpennies and farthings, to canvass from house to house, night after night, in storm, in rain, in tempest or when the atmosphere in the alleys and byways they visited was well-nigh asphyxiating.

A. J. Greenberg

It is a ridiculous scheme to spend a sum of upwards of a quarter of a million pounds to provide a Hospital for the few Jews who cannot talk English or do not care to.

Viscount Knutsford

The
Social Background

INTRODUCTION

One day, in January 1907, a group of immigrant, Yiddish-speaking working men, met in the kitchen of a basement flat in Sydney Street, Stepney, in the East End of London.[1] Their leader was Isador Berliner,[2] a barber, who had come to this country from Russia in 1891. He told his colleagues that he wanted to build a hospital that would be under Jewish management, and staffed by Jewish doctors and Jewish nurses. Those present formed themselves into a committee, made a collection totalling one shilling and sixpence,[3] and determined to call a public meeting to forward this aim. Who were these men? What was their background? And why did they want a specifically Jewish hospital? What section of the community were they trying to help? Was such a hospital needed, and would they find support or opposition from the wealthier Jews? If they met with opposition, how could they raise sufficient money to buy a site, erect a hospital, and fund the running costs?

At that time, even internationally-renowned voluntary hospitals in London with handsome endowments, such as Guy's, St Thomas's, and St Bartholomew's, were experiencing the greatest difficulty in surviving financially. The cost of treatment was rising inexorably due to the availability of more sophisticated equipment and medicine, and the heightened expectation of patients. Hospitals were closing down beds, wards and sometimes whole wings, and there was talk that due to lack of sufficient public support the London Hospital would have to close down completely.[4] Throughout the voluntary hospital world the cry was for more money.

In that situation, for these East Enders, with their one shilling and sixpence capital, to believe that they could succeed in building, and then maintaining, a new hospital supported by public subscriptions was to indulge in an impossible dream. Their Sydney Street meeting was to lead to a David and Goliath confrontation, with Lord Rothschild cast as Goliath and Berliner in the role of David.

3

RUSSIA AND POLAND – THE SOURCE OF LATE NINETEENTH CENTURY JEWISH IMMIGRATION INTO ENGLAND

There were about 35,000 Jews in London in 1870, a high proportion of whom had arrived from Holland and Germany in the previous fifty years. From 1870 onward there was a steady stream of immigrant Jews from Russia and Poland,[1] but the assassination of Tsar Alexander II on 1 March 1881 brought about a dramatic change; the stream of immigration became a raging flood. By 1900 there were more than 100,000 Jews living in the East End of London alone,[2] mostly in Aldgate and Whitechapel, but also in Mile End, Stepney, and Bethnal Green. Almost all the newcomers came from the Pale of Settlement, the fifteen western and southern provinces of Russia and the Kingdom of Poland in which, by law, Jews were confined. Others followed from Austro-Hungary (mainly Galicia) and Romania.

It was from this post-1881 group of immigrants that Berliner drew his main support, and it was principally for their benefit that he desired a Jewish hospital. Their Russian and Polish backgrounds were an important factor in this story.

Life was never easy for Jews in Russia; its government was arbitrary, authoritarian and persecutory. One of the greatest hardships Jews faced was that conditions alternated violently back and forth between periods of relative tolerance and calm and periods of reaction and repression, depending upon who was occupying the throne. This led to a continuous state of insecurity, fed and sustained by popular violence, propaganda, and discrimination. Memories of this insecurity travelled with the emigrating Jews, and manifested itself in a distrust of anything official, particularly established institutions that threatened their fundamental beliefs and freedom.

The reign of the tyrannical and merciless Nicholas I between 1825 and 1855 was especially savage. Under his jurisdiction more than six hundred anti-Jewish edicts were written into law. These ranged from the mildly annoying – censorship of Jewish texts and newspapers and rules that restricted the curricula of Jewish schools; to the monstrous – expulsion from homes and villages, confiscation of property, and a decree binding boys from the ages of twelve to twenty-five to service in the Russian army for twenty-five years. The object of this Iron Tsar was to remove all traces of Judaism from his Tsardom; to purify and Christianise it.

The accession of Alexander II in 1855 came as a relief. He was advised by his ministers that restrictions on Jews were not only unjust, but harmful to Russia's economic interests, and concessions were made. He permitted some Jewish youths to enter Russian universities. A few Jewish businessmen whom he found useful were allowed to travel in parts of Russia where they had previously been prohibited. There was a modest relaxation of the heavy Jewish taxes, and the period of compulsory conscription was reduced to five years. But the reign of his successor, Alexander III, was marked by relentless hostility. Like Nicholas I, Alexander III had a fanatical resolve to eradicate Judaism as a religious entity. His 'May Laws' of 1882 prohibited Jews from owning or renting land outside towns and cities, discouraged them from living in villages, and prohibited them from engaging in work on Sundays and Christian holidays. In that year 500,000 Jews in rural areas were forced to leave their homes and live in towns or townlets (*shtetls*) in the Pale, resulting in intolerable overcrowding and fewer economic opportunities. By the end of the century forty per cent of Jews in the Pale were living wholly or partly on charity, and it was said of Vilna that fully eighty per cent of its Jewish population did not know in the evening how and where they would obtain food the next morning.

Though only one of the five conspirators responsible for Alexander II's death was Jewish, (a young seamstress named Jessie Helfmann, later hanged), the Jews were blamed. There was an attack on Jews at Elisavetgrad, and a wave of terror spread through the provinces of Kiev, Chernigov, Poltava, Kherson and Ekaterinoslav. Pogroms started in the Ukraine and continued sporadically until 1884, mainly confined to Southern Russia. Four years later Jews were forbidden to move from one village to another without a special permit. In 1891 they were expelled from Moscow and Kiev, and in 1899 an economic crisis in Bessarabia and Kherson led to famine and riots. There were further pogroms in 1903 in Kishinev, followed by one of the worst, in Odessa, in 1905.

For Jews, the Pale of Settlement had become a land of severe social deprivation and religious persecution, and they were forced to think of emigration. Between 1880–1914 there was an exodus of more than two million Jews from Russia to the United States, Britain, other parts of Europe, South America and Palestine. They decided to leave in order to escape the pogroms, (or fear of them), the grinding poverty, a corrupt bureaucracy, and the restrictions on their lives. They left because they were hungry, because they were persecuted, because life in Russia had become intolerable.

To quit the place they grew up in, some having to leave a wife and children behind to be sent for later, to strike out for a distant seaport, taking steerage passage in what were often insanitary boats, for a country whose language they could not speak and where most of them knew no-one, meant it was the more enterprising and determined person, with a strong individualistic attitude, who was likely to be predominant amongst them. This was a quality that would be much needed by Berliner and his supporters.

Most immigrants to England landed in London. They brought with them only a little money – (the majority arrived at the Port of London with ten shillings or less a head) – and a few tools of their trade. They brought with them harsh memories of oppression and economic deprivation, but they also brought with them hope, and a determination to provide a better life for themselves and their families.

THE ESTABLISHED COMMUNITY
AND THE NEWCOMERS

The history of the London Jewish Hospital illustrates many of the intricate patterns of relationship between the existing Anglo-Jewish community and the new arrivals.

The leadership of the community was drawn from 'the Cousinhood', an upper and upper-middle class of some two hundred families, largely linked by marriage, such as the Rothschilds, Goldsmids, Cohens, Montefiores, Salomons, Mocattas, Henriques, Josephs, Franklins, Samuels and Montagus. They lived near one another and mixed socially in both Jewish and non-Jewish circles. They had led the community's struggle to obtain full civic emancipation, and assumed the leading role in setting up and controlling the community's voluntary bodies – synagogal, particularly the United Synagogue and the Reform Synagogue; representative, such as the Board of Deputies of British Jews; educational, being the main financial supporters of the Jewish schools; and philanthropic, covering every aspect of welfare.

During the nineteenth century the community leaders created a mini-welfare state with a network of efficient Jewish organisations that supplemented the general Poor Law system. There was a society for providing for the wants of the Jewish poor at every stage from the cradle to the grave. Though today they might be considered parsimonious, by Victorian standards they were generous. There were Jewish loan societies, soup kitchens, clothing associations, and societies for the distribution of bread and fuel tickets. The Jewish Blind Society was established as early as 1819, and the *Jewish Chronicle* claimed in 1842 that 'now, happily, there does not remain in the metropolis a single blind Jew requiring aid without a stipend for life'. The Jews' Deaf and Dumb Home opened in 1865; a Home and Hospital for Jewish Incurables at Nightingale Lane, Tottenham in 1889; and a convalescent home for tuberculosis sufferers at Daneswood in 1905.

The Jewish Board of Guardians, established in 1859, dominated the scene. Operating from Middlesex Street, (better known as Petticoat Lane), it engaged in effective sanitary work; was active in preventing the spread of tuberculosis; arranged apprenticeships; made small loans to enable men to start in business; hired sewing machines to tailors; and gave many other types of relief to those most in need.

The system provided a cushion against the problems of everyday life with which the Jewish poor had to contend. And, most importantly, as will be discussed, special arrangements were made by the Cousinhood to ensure adequate medical and hospital care for the Jewish sick poor.

The establishment's acceptance of responsibility was motivated by a mixture of noblesse oblige, ethnic sympathies, a firm belief in the Victorian ethos of voluntary effort in charity work, and self-interest. It was self-interest, which does not necessarily imply selfishness, that caused them to fear that their hard-won political and social gains could be irrevocably damaged by the newcomers who brought with them not only their bedding, their cutlery, and their crockery, but also their own way of life. Established Jews viewed the newcomers with a mixture of sympathy and alarm, and feared that the sheer numbers involved might encourage the anti-Semitism that was increasing in English society in the late 1870s.[1] There were rumblings of discontent against the newcomers even among working-class Jews.

The Cousinhood's patrician role survived into the twentieth century. However, like their contemporaries, they were anxious not to create what today might be called a benefit dependency culture outlook, and Jewish charities, particularly the Jewish Board of Guardians, aimed to make every Jewish citizen, as far as possible, a self-supporting and self-respecting member of society.

Controlling the Influx

Until the great influx began, the community was relatively compact and well organised in its communal life, and by 1880 its full integration into English society was in sight. The staggering increase in numbers after 1881 brought about a situation of an altogether different dimension; the existing Jewish community was swamped and severe problems ensued.

The view was frequently expressed that three generations would have to pass before the foreign Jew became fully integrated, but now a completely new generation had arrived, almost in an instant, and communal leaders were apprehensive that the machinery of relief they had set up would be overwhelmed. The lifeboat was full; they feared it would capsize with its passengers if more tried to clamber aboard. The new immigrants were perhaps more independent and less subservient than their predecessors, and could not be so easily moulded and controlled. Their insistence on maintaining their own way of life caused friction, and led to the formation of institutions that more closely matched their needs.

8

The establishment attempted to control the influx with a triple strategy. First, they tried to dissuade further newcomers from setting out from the Pale. The Jewish Board of Guardians placed advertisements in the Jewish press in Poland and Russia warning of the economic hardships that faced the newcomer, and paid for some immigrants to return to the *heim* and for others to go on to America and the Colonies. Even the Chief Rabbi, Nathan Marcus Adler, lent his voice; he urged rabbis in eastern Europe to warn their congregants not to travel to England because, he told them, English charities could not cope, and difficulty in finding sufficient work was causing many men to violate the Sabbath and the holy days, and was driving them into the ensnaring net of Christian missionaries seeking converts.[2]

This tactic had only limited success and was short-lived. Once it was clear that immigration would continue and that, once here, the newcomers were determined to stay, not only were they accepted, but the Jewish establishment championed the right of those remaining in Russia and Poland who wished to come to England to be allowed to enter as refugees from religious oppression. Samuel Montagu defended the immigrants before the Royal Commission on Alien Immigration in 1903, and Lord Rothschild, a member of the Commission, opposed restriction of any kind.

When Hermann Adler preached at Princelet Street Synagogue on the occasion of the celebration of its refurbishment on 26 March 1893[3] he impressed upon the working class congregation that they too should support their brethren 'who have newly arrived here from the country where they have been so cruelly oppressed and so heartlessly persecuted'. He asked:

> Shall we join the hue and cry which is raised in certain quarters and signify our assent to any measures that may prevent the immigration of 'destitute aliens' as they are called? ... No my brethren, emphatically no! Our conduct is clearly prescribed by the words of the Torah (Exodus XXII.9). 'Thou shalt not oppress a stranger for ye know the heart of a stranger seeing that you were strangers in the land of Egypt'. Selfishness, lack of sympathy with those wretched outcasts is altogether unworthy of a human being. With us Jews it should be altogether inexplicable.

He reminded them that the time was not long past when they themselves passed anxious lives within 'the inhospitable lands of the north'.

The second strand of the Cousinhood's strategy was to integrate the immigrants into English life and society as quickly as possible. The *Jewish Chronicle* considered this to be a matter of the utmost urgency:[4]

The foreign poor form a community within the community. They come mostly from Poland; they, as it were, bring Poland with them, and they retain Poland while they stop here. This is most undesirable: it is more than a misfortune, it is a calamity. Our outside world is not capable of making minute discrimination between Jew and Jew, and forms its opinion of Jews in general as much, if not more, from them than from the Anglicized portion of the community. We are then responsible for them.

Integration became the top priority. Lay, ecclesiastical, educational, and philanthropic resources were mobilised for a crash course in Englishness. It cannot be too strongly emphasised, however, that neither the schools nor the leaders of the community required any sacrifice of religious beliefs on the part of the newcomers; they did not encourage religious assimilation. Integration was the object, and pride in being Jewish was promoted to the fullest extent. Baron Ferdinand de Rothschild told the children of Stepney Jewish Schools, 'never forget so long as you live that you are Jews and Jewesses'.

The schools, Jewish and non-Jewish, were the main vehicles for integration; but initially it was the East End Jewish voluntary charity schools, led by Jews' Free School, that bore the brunt of the task. At the turn of the century, JFS had more than 4,250 pupils and was the largest school in the world.[5] The *Jewish Chronicle* boasted that a young Pole could be placed in the JFS with the assurance that at the end of his training he would be turned out a young Englishman. The Board of Trade Report of 1894 into the effects of immigration was a little more circumspect, noting that immigrant children emerged from JFS *almost* indistinguishable from English children.

The three main areas that caused tension and contention between the two groups were religious observance, the use of Yiddish, and the provision of medical care.

Many newcomers considered the official religious organisations of Anglo-Jewry unsatisfactory. They had weighed up the orthodoxy of the United Synagogue and found it wanting, and were prepared openly to repudiate it. The minority who were aware of the existence and beliefs of the Chief Rabbi had little regard for him. They came from self-governing communities, each with its own rabbi, and the Chief Rabbi's office was alien to their East European experience. They shunned the coldness of the United Synagogue's lofty cathedral-like structures with their stained glass windows and massive pillars, and preferred to meet and worship in their own small, noisy, sometimes scruffy, informal synagogues – their *stiebles* – that were open at all times of the day, and in which they felt comfortable and at ease. They came to these hotbeds of Judaism to pray, or study, or chat, or a combination of all three. They came, wrote Israel Zangwill in *Children of the Ghetto*,[6] 'two or often three times a day to batter the gates of heaven. They dropped in, mostly in their workaday garments and grime, and rumbled and roared and chorused prayers with a zeal that shook the window-panes. It supplied them not only with their religion, but their arts and letters, their politics and their public amusements. It was their home as well as the Almighty's'.

It was the difference in atmosphere of the *stiebles* compared with that of the established synagogues that was important to the new immigrants. They had a warmth, a *heimische* ambiance, of a kind that they desired, but did not find, for example, when they were unfortunate enough to have to go into hospital. Rev W. Esterson, the Minister at the Hambro Synagogue, said[7] that experience showed the newcomers were never so happy as when they were in Jewish surroundings; they felt the lack of a Jewish heart and Jewish sympathy most strongly in troublesome times of sickness and suffering.

For most of the older newcomers their first, and sometimes only language was Yiddish, a remarkable composite tongue that could be a mixture of Polish and Hebrew, of German and Hebrew, or of Latvian and Hebrew, or a combination of all of them. The elite disliked Yiddish, a dislike stemming from the belief that its continued use could keep immigrants isolated from the English community. For Moses Angel, headmaster of the JFS from 1842 to 1898, it was redolent of all that he considered undesirable in foreign ways and habits. Weaning his pupils away from it as quickly as possible, and substituting well-spoken English, was seen as an essential first step. Samuel Montagu (later Lord Swaythling) asked pupils to refuse to learn Yiddish from their parents; instead, they should teach their parents to speak English. The efforts of the schools brought their reward. A reporter from the *Daily Graphic* who visited JFS in 1895 wrote, 'When they leave, they all speak English with a regard for grammar and a purity of accent far above the average of the neighbourhood'.

Despite all attempts to discourage its use the older immigrants preferred it. Shop signs, posters and advertisements were in Yiddish, and there was a thriving Yiddish Theatre at the Pavilion in Whitechapel Road where comedies and dramas, many based on Jewish experience in the Pale, were performed, the actors' repertory extending to opera by Verdi and plays by Shakespeare. A Yiddish Theatre performance was as much ritual as conventional drama – a celebration of a shared language, culture and identity, in some ways almost akin to a religious service. Attending such performances gave an added communal unity and cohesion to its immigrant audience who looked forward to the weekend performances 'as a pious man waits for the Sabbath'.[8]

The community set up a network of clubs and societies catering for both adults and young people, all of which had the underlying aim of achieving integration.

Typical were the Jewish Working Men's Club (founded by Samuel Montagu in 1872), the Jewish Girls' Club (established by Lady Magnus in 1886), the West Central Jewish Girls' Club (established by Montagu's daughter, Lily, in 1893), and the Brady Boys' Club (founded in Whitechapel under Lady Rothschild's patronage in 1896). The Jewish Lads' Brigade, founded in 1895 by Colonel A E W Goldsmid, was modelled on the Church Lads' Brigade, whose quasi-militaristic and religiously patriotic spirit it unashamedly followed. While children made the transition into English ways very readily, their parents found it less easy.

Because of concern that the concentration of Jews in such a small area would encourage anti-Semitism to flourish and provide anti-alienists with the ammunition they needed to stop the flow of immigration, the third strand of the Cousinhood's strategy was an attempt to disperse the community more widely, to empty the 'ghetto'. The Russo-Jewish Committee established offices to assist immigrants to move to other areas, and attempts were even made to settle Jews on land near Colchester where they would raise cattle and sheep to provide meat for the kosher market. Under the patronage of Samuel Montagu, the Jewish Dispersion Committee was established in 1903 with the aim of relocating some of the more anglicized immigrants to smaller cities, such as Reading, where Jewish communal facilities existed, but it made comparatively little headway.

Berliner and his friends were grateful for the support they received from the established Jewish community, but preferred institutions like the *stiebles* that more closely reflected the desires of the newcomers. Where a gap existed in the system, as they believed was the case with the hospitals, they were prepared to fill it for themselves.

THE EAST END IN 1900

In 1900, there were some 15,000 Jews, mainly poor, living in the West End of London, mostly in Soho and Fitzrovia.[1] A comparative few were to be found in South London. The wealthy, and most of the middle class, were in Mayfair, Marylebone, Bayswater, Maida Vale and St John's Wood, but it was the East End that was the magnet for the overwhelming majority of London's Jewish poor. Once the original settlement had taken root there in the seventeenth century, later arrivals joined them. The principal attractions of the East End for the recently arrived immigrants were the availability of housing and work, and an existing community that catered specifically for their needs.

By 1900, many of the streets in Aldgate and Whitechapel, such as Brick Lane, Middlesex Street, Wentworth Street, Fashion Street, Flower and Dean Street, Thrawl Street, Old Montague Street, Chicksand Street and Hanbury Street to the north of Whitechapel Road, and Plumbers Row and Greenfield Street south of Whitechapel Road – were, to all intents and purposes 100% Jewish.[2]

Many of the Gentile-dominated streets that surrounded them were strongholds of London labourers, mostly Irish, many of them dockers and railwaymen, who would have no dealings with the Jews and would not live with them. Broken windows and other forcible arguments were frequently used to convince the unlucky Jew who had the temerity to take up residence in these streets, that for him, at least, they were not desirable homes.

The district was amongst the most congested in London and overcrowding was rife, largely caused by the demolition of insanitary housing that was partly being replaced by warehouses and factories. There were, on average, fourteen residents per house in 1900. An investigation carried out by *The Lancet* in 1884 found a Jewish potato dealer who kept his wife, five children, and a huge stock of potatoes all in one room measuring five yards by six. There was just one bed. Some of the worst cases of insanitary accommodation and overcrowding were in Old Montague Street, Booth Street, Hanbury Street and Chicksand Street. Most families had just one or two rooms, often shared with a lodger, and one room frequently doubled as a workshop for a tailoring father.

It must be emphasised that even before 1900 not all poor Jews lived in such unsatisfactory conditions, and at their worst the immigrant dwellings in the East End were never as unwholesome as the pestholes of Limehouse, Paddington or Camberwell. Jews did not inhabit the poorest of the Spitalfields rookeries that were the breeding grounds of epidemics and crime; instead, they paid high rents for rooms in 'houses of sunken eminence, once occupied by well-paid skilled workers, or even by the merchant classes who had moved elsewhere as the neighbourhood slowly declined'.[3]

Housing conditions progressively, though gradually, improved. Many Jews lived in very much better accommodation in nearby Georgian squares. The 'model dwellings' created in the 1890's by Lord Rothschild's Four Percent Industrial Dwellings Company in Flower & Dean Street, and by the East End Dwellings Company in Thrawl Street, provided solid and sanitary accommodation at a fair rent. A goodly proportion of the surrounding streets boasted houses that despite infinite partitions had rooms with high ceilings and large windows. New Road, Prescott Street, Great Alie Street and others had well-built and even handsome accommodation. On Stepney Green, there were, and still are, fine Queen Anne mansions. In Great Prescott Street and in Wellclose Square were houses which, with renovation, could match the houses of Mayfair.

Despite its disadvantages – and they were many – the East End was well provided with the necessities of Jewish life, and death; Jewish schools, shopkeepers selling kosher food, more than one hundred synagogues, and four burial grounds within easy distance. In Petticoat Lane, Wentworth Street, and Brick Lane, there was scarcely a shop or stall that was not Jewish owned. The names above the shops were of Cohen, Pomerantz, Frumkin, Toporovski, Pinkus, Spielsinger, Proops, Domb, Petrikoski and similar. Streets were thronged with Jewish shoppers, and contained everything for their daily needs, the small grocery shops permeated with the smell of pickled herring, garlic sausage, and onion bread, and the sellers of live chickens doing a steady trade. It was an area full of meeting places – Jewish clubs, societies, cafes and restaurants – a self-contained milieu that encompassed a whole range of social and cultural life in which people spoke of Warsaw, Kishinev, Kiev and Odessa as if they were neighbouring suburbs.

To visitors, it was like entering a foreign land. 'We have entered an alien world', wrote Henry Walker in 1896. 'It is in the heart of London, yet like a foreign town with its own trade, its own segregated peoples, religion, customs and industries'.[4] 'I doubt', said Mrs Brewer, writing in 1892,[5] 'if there is any place in the wide world that contains so much of intense human interest as exists in Whitechapel'.

Russell and Lewis, in their 1900 book *The Jew in London*, noted that alongside the overcrowding, the most conspicuous features of this Jewish colony were sobriety and hard work:

> Yet, strange as it may seem, this great and largely squalid colony is a peaceful and law-abiding population. On the larger scale it may even be said to be a moral population. Drunkenness is almost unknown; temperance societies are unheard of, for the Jew is never intoxicated. Public-houses will be full on Saturday and Sunday night, but not a Jewish face will be seen there. Personal violence towards women is almost unknown. Licentiousness among women is equally rare. Family ties are sacred. Considering that Whitechapel is overwhelmingly a colony of aliens, the consequences, socially and politically, might have been serious; a disaffected people might have been a standing menace to London ... Happily, nothing, in fact, is more remarkable on Sunday than the orderliness of a great population of aliens in faith and speech ... who are, it must be said, less aggressive in the streets than many of their better circumstanced co-residents.

Because accommodation was limited and families were large, the streets became a communal leisure resource. Throbbing with life, they provided a fascinating and exciting mixture.[6] The broad promenade of Whitechapel Road, still one of the widest streets in London, was the gathering ground, breathing space, market, and discussion forum of the immigrant Jews. On a fine Sunday evening in Whitechapel, all the shops were open and the restaurants busy. Off Whitechapel Road, at every quarter mile or so, was an unusual side street to catch the interest, and in the midst of the shops a herd of cows – a kosher dairy farm.

As for available work, the East End was a centre of typical Jewish immigrant occupations – tailoring, boot and shoe making, the fur trade, cabinet making, and the tobacco trade. This made the area attractive even for the 'greeners', the newest of newcomers.

However inferior his early accommodation might be, however poorly paid his first employment, the new arrival could stay within the womb provided by this environment until he had mastered the English language and acquired sufficient funds to move on, though the Yiddish-speaking community was so large, and so socially self-contained that, for the adult immigrant, there was little necessity to move or even to learn English should he not wish to put himself to the trouble.

To the Jewish immigrant, especially the more elderly, being in the East End meant to be able to live as they had in the *shtetl*, but without the brutal attentions of a hostile government.

INTRODUCTION

[1] The venue of this meeting according to Mrs A Levy, *Jewish Chronicle* 9 May 1919.

[2] Also sometimes described as Isadore or Isaac.

[3] *Jewish Chronicle*, 29 November 1912.

[4] The threat came close to reality in 1920 when Viscount Knutsford, Chairman of the Hospital, declared closure was inevitable unless there was a dramatic reversal of the Hospital's financial fortune. 'It is impossible to keep silent, because unless largely helped, the London Hospital cannot pay its expenses after the end of this month, something I thought I would never have to say after 25 years of strenuous and almost daily work. *Jewish World*, 22 June 1920.

RUSSIA AND POLAND – THE SOURCE OF LATE NINETEENTH CENTURY JEWISH IMMIGRATION INTO ENGLAND

[1] *Russo-Jewish Immigrants in England before 1881.* A. R. Rollin in *Transactions of the Jewish Historical Society of England.* XXI p. 202–213.

[2] For further details of the Jewish population in nineteenth century London see *Jewish Chronicle*, 2 June 1876; Lipman, *Social History*, pp. 65+, 99+; Joseph Jacobs, *Studies in Jewish Statistics*, 1891, first published in the *Jewish Chronicle* in 1883; Lloyd Gartner *The Jewish Immigrant in England 1870–1914* (1960) See also Appendix A of C. Russell and H. L. Lewis *The Jew in London* (1900), and John Gerrard, *The English and Immigration*, Appendix A.

THE ESTABLISHED COMMUNITY AND THE NEWCOMERS

[1] Colin Holmes. *Anti-Semitism in British Society 1876–1939.* New York (1979).

[2] *HaMelix XXVIII 287*, 30 December 1888; and see further sources quoted in Lloyd Gartner at pp. 23, 25.

[3] Quoted in *Giant among Giants* (1994) Samuel C. Melnick p. 75.

[4] *Jewish Chronicle* 12 December 1881.

[5] *JFS. The History of the Jews' Free School, London since 1732.* (1998) Gerry Black.

[6] Published in 1892.

[7] *Jewish World*, 17 June 1914.

[8] See article by David Mazower in *Jewish Chronicle* colour magazine, 26 June 1987 and his monograph *Yiddish Theatre in London* (1987).

THE EAST END IN 1900

[1] See *Living Up West. Jewish Life in London's West End* (1994) Gerry Black.

[2] There is a map of Jewish East London in *The Jew in London* (1900) by C. Russell and H. S. Lewis indicating street by street the percentage of Jewish inhabitants. Copies of the map can be purchased from the Jewish Museum in London.

[3] Lloyd Gartner, *The Jewish Immigrant in England 1870–1914* (1973) p. 143.

[4] Henry Walker. *East London* 1896.

[5] *The Jewish Colony in London*, in The Sunday Magazine XXI pp. 10–20, 119–23, quoted in *A Documentary History of Jewish Immigrants in Britain 1840–1920* (1994) David Englander.

[6] *The Real East End*. Thomas Burke. 1932.

The
Medical Background

JEWISH COMMUNITY CARE
FOR ITS SICK POOR BEFORE 1880

The manner in which a community deals with its sick poor is a good measure of its humanity, its *rachmones*, its own moral health. To help the sick is a *mitzvah* that involves both rich and poor, for infection is no respecter of persons. As the Haham, Dr Moses Gaster, said:[1]

> The boon of satisfactory health concerns the wealthy and the less wealthy members of the community alike. Assume for a moment that there are no hospitals at all; what would be the position of the well-to-do? They would be faced with a terrible cause of infection, and for their own sakes would have to take upon themselves the task of helping the poor sufferers.

It was inevitable that the crucial role in promoting health care for the Jewish poor in London would be played by the wealthy, for there was no other section of the community so fitted or capable to undertake the task. They supplied the money and took control of the institutions carrying out the work. The poor contributed too, sometimes giving more, pro rata, than the middle class, but with just one or two notable exceptions their payments were but a small proportion of the required total.

As early as 1660, the Sephardi community employed a physician to attend upon its sick poor and provide medicines; the office of 'Physician to the Community' became a permanent feature from 1673 onwards.[2] The community established a society in 1747 to erect a hospital, and after seeking advice from the London Hospital opened the Beth Holim in Leman Street the following year. It later moved to Mile End Road, and is now a residential care home in Wembley, Middlesex. Similarly, from the 1720s, the dignitaries of the Ashkenazi Great Synagogue included a physician, at a salary of £30 per annum, whose duty it was to look after the sick poor.

For many years medical provision for the Ashkenazi poor was in the joint hands of the Great, the New, and the Hambro Synagogues. Their appointed doctor saw patients who came to his surgery, where he dispensed his own medicines. He also paid visits to the homes of those living within a one mile radius of Duke's Place, thus covering the area inhabited by the vast majority of the Jewish poor. In the 1850s he attended between 3,000 and 4,000 patients a year, and as London's Jewish population was then about 25,000, this represented a substantial provision of free medical attendance, superior to that then available to the majority of London's poor.

The executive of the New Synagogue suggested to the Great and the Hambro that responsibility for medical relief should be transferred from the synagogues to the newly established Jewish Board of Guardians, and, in 1861, the Board undertook the task.[3] Two years later its medical officers were able to report:[4]

> The aggregate amount of disease among the Jewish poor under our care is very much decreased compared with the preceding year ... it is a matter of congratulation that the mortality among our patients has been considerably below the general average. Cleanliness, formerly so much neglected, especially among the foreign poor, is beginning to be valued for its own sake.

The Board soon discovered, as governments have found to their despair ever since, that it is extremely difficult to control the cost of medical care. The numbers calling upon its services quickly rose, and the Board believed it was being taken advantage of by those who could well afford to pay for their own medicines. It was noted that nearly all the applicants who had resorted to the Board's dispensary also applied for free medicine elsewhere. It was common, among Jewish and non-Jewish patients, to attend a Poor Law doctor, a free dispensary, and the doctor in charge of a hospital out-patient department all for the same ailment. In this way, they had three bottles of medicine from three different doctors, and took a draught from one in the morning, from the second in the middle of the day, and from the third in the evening.[5]

In its Annual Report of 1870, the Board said that many who called upon the doctor had complaints of the most trivial character. Administrative measures were taken to reduce the numbers, but costs continued to soar. So the Board instigated an enquiry into the efficiency of the alternative free services provided by doctors employed by the local authorities, and found them to be adequate. It was preparing the ground to justify the termination of its own medical service.

In August 1873, it was decided that outdoor medical relief should be 'tentatively' discontinued for three months. It never resumed. In 1879, 'a fresh and clear principle' was enunciated – 'there being nothing of a specifically Jewish character in the mere dispensing of drugs and the giving of medical advice, the Board has resolved to avail itself of the facilities given by the State for this purpose – a scheme that has long been in contemplation'.[6] It resolved 'to substitute the medical relief provided by the state for the special medical relief provided by the Board'. So it was, that immediately before the massive influx of the 1880s, one of the strands of Jewish medical care was removed.

However, other communal support remained in place. Jewish institutions were particularly effective in caring for mothers and children, and were often in the vanguard of progress. A Jewish Day Nursery was opened in Spitalfields in 1897, moving to New Road in 1901. It had excellent facilities, was run on up-to-date hygienic lines, and was one of the best of the few such nurseries in London. It was a special boon to working mothers and widower fathers.

Mrs Alice Model, nee Sichel [1856–1943] started the Sick Room Helps Society in January 1895 with Miss Bella Lowy at a time when general maternity services were minimal.[7] It arranged for women to take the place of the mother in the home at a time when, by reason of confinement or illness, she was unable to cope by herself. The helpers washed the baby, got the other children ready and sent them to school, cooked the food, tidied and cleaned up the home, and took care of the washing. Lady Samuel described them as 'scientific charwomen'. It gave the mother peace of mind, as well as helped her physical recovery, for she knew that her husband and children were well cared for. With the financial assistance of Lady Rothschild, F. D. Mocatta, Sir Julian Goldsmid, and a few other friends, two trained nurses were employed.

In 1897 the Society started a provident section, 'to encourage self-respect and thrift'. The subscription was one penny a week, and in Mrs Model's words, 'the paying members of the Society are not simply beneficiaries of a charitable institution, but a combine of women for mutual help'. By 1904 the Society had six trained nurses and thirty-six helps, each case attended being nursed for a fortnight. By 1908, there were 3,700 provident members.

A Jewish Maternity Home was opened in Underwood Street in September 1911 that later became a recognised training school for midwives. Adjoining land was purchased, and in November 1927 an enlarged maternity home with fourteen beds was officially opened by Lord Reading. In 1933 there were nearly 800 births at the Home. Thereafter the numbers declined, as did the general birth rate, and as, indeed, did the Jewish population of the East End.[8]

All Jewish births in Stepney were notified to Jewish care organisations by Stepney Borough Council, and the organisations sent health visitors to the homes to persuade mothers to bring their children in for supervision. It was rare for a Jewish child in need to be overlooked by the system. Mrs Model was able to claim[9] that in the midst of the Jewish area in Whitechapel a complete maternity and child welfare centre had been established that was considered a model of its kind by the authorities.

There was of course no National Health Service at the end of the nineteenth century, but wide-ranging health services, charitable and governmental, were available. London was better supplied with medical services than the rest of England, and the East End of London better supplied than the rest of London. Because the Jewish community provided additional medical help, if you had to be Jewish, poor, and ill, the East End was a good place to be.

THE VOLUNTARY HOSPITALS AND THE INFIRMARIES

At the beginning of the twentieth century, the available choice of hospitals, insofar as the patient had a choice, lay between the municipal poor law infirmaries that were funded out of the rates by the Poor Law Guardians, and the voluntary hospitals that relied mainly on charitable donations, or as Viscount Knutsford, Chairman of the London Hospital described it, were 'dependent on the energy of some maniac in begging'.[1]

The voluntary hospitals effectively depended almost entirely upon the willingness of the rich to help the poor. Speaking at the annual meeting of the King's Fund in 1906, the Duke of Fife said 'the plain truth is that the London hospitals are maintained by a small number of charitable people'. Knutsford said it was the voluntary system that provided the principal teaching hospitals on which the public depended for their doctors and nurses. 'All progress in medicine and surgery has been made in the voluntary hospitals, and hardly anywhere else. There is in them the elasticity of management which is essential to progress'.[3]

Victorian society distinguished between the poor and the destitute. The function of the Poor Law was to relieve destitution; the object of the voluntary hospitals was to prevent it, by stepping in to grant free medical relief to the provident and thrifty who, through no fault of their own, met with an accident or were overtaken by disease.

London's voluntary hospitals were founded to provide care for the sick poor. The oldest, St Bartholomew's (founded in 1123) and St Thomas's (1207), were well endowed, benefitting from the income of estates confiscated from the Church by Henry VIII. Several new hospitals were built in the first half of the eighteenth century – Westminster (1720); Guy's (1724); St George's (1733); the London (1741); and the Middlesex (1745). They were followed, between 1818 and 1856, by Charing Cross, King's College, St Mary's, University College, and the Royal Free Hospitals.[3] Their founders were usually persons of high standing in their local communities, and their governors were persons at the top, or keen to approach the top, of the social pyramid.

By 1900, London's voluntary hospitals were treating two million patients a year and spending one million pounds in maintaining ten thousand beds for in-patients. In contrast, in Continental Europe and America most hospitals were maintained by the state or municipalities. It was generally accepted that the English voluntary system was then unsurpassed by any other hospital system in the world, in efficiency, equipment, administration, and economy. By the standards of the time, they provided a high quality of care.[4]

It was said in favour of the voluntary hospitals that because they had to compete for financial support they were more efficient in administration, more critical in analysing the performance of the work done by everyone from senior physician to the humblest official, and were more likely to treat their patients as human beings. It was contended that in municipal hospitals the absence of competition made for inefficiency, and whereas ill-managed voluntary hospitals would lose their support and have to close down, inefficient municipal hospitals continued to exist, their administration became overmanned and lax, and their work indifferent. But the voluntary hospitals lacked co-operation one with the other, had no overall comprehensive plan, and were finding it increasingly difficult to raise sufficient monies. Despite this, it was believed at the time that a complete state takeover of the voluntary hospitals would be a grave evil.[5]

Though their revenues were rising, voluntary hospitals developed an increased need to spend. Their financial health varied widely, between a small surplus and a worrying deficit. Despite some enormous individual bequests, few hospitals were augmenting their capital; most were sliding further and further into debt. Only the three endowed hospitals, Guy's, Bart's, and St Thomas's, had substantial reserves, but even Guy's began to suffer financial embarrassment from the 1880s onwards due to the collapse in the value of its agricultural estates. There never was a period when the voluntary hospitals were free from financial worry.

The principal sources of funding for the voluntary hospitals were contributions made by the public, in the form of donations, legacies and subscriptions; dividends from such investments as they had; street collections; and, later, payments by patients who could afford something towards the cost of their treatment. Some contribution was made by the Poor Law authorities when they requested voluntary hospitals to treat paupers.

Hospitals could also look to the three London Hospital Funds, all of which survive today and remain active. The Metropolitan Hospital Sunday Fund, launched at the Mansion House in 1873, was essentially a middle and upper class dominated organisation that raised money through special church and synagogue collections in June each year. Church collections had traditionally been used to benefit hospitals; the Sunday Fund co-ordinated and distributed them more effectively. It acted along the lines of a central hospital board, gathering information, making hospital visits, and giving money to those institutions it thought were doing beneficial work. By the mid-1890s, it was collecting about £40,000 a year from over 1,800 congregations.

The Hospital Saturday Fund, established in 1874, raised money from the working classes, largely through workshop, factory and street collections on pay days. In London, its annual receipts totalled about £20,000. Though it lacked the Sunday Fund's social connections and knowledge of hospital administration, it developed a method of allocating funds based on hospital efficiency, and expected to have a say in the running of the institutions it supported.

The King Edward VII Hospital Fund for London, founded in 1897 to honour Queen Victoria's sixty years on the throne, was originally named The Prince of Wales Hospital Fund for London, and is now called The King's Fund. It distributed by far the most[6] and aimed to make good the annual deficits of London's voluntary hospitals.

Despite help from the three funds, the hospitals were compelled to make continuous appeals and launch publicity campaigns. The leading fundraiser, and staunchest champion of the voluntary hospital system, was Viscount Knutsford. He said that 50,000 personal letters produced only 2,500 answers, and in his experience one mile of writing raised £200. Regular subscribers were courted and flattered, and subscription lists invariably published. Even the endowed hospitals were finding it necessary to make public appeals, and their entry into the field made life yet more difficult for the others.

The strong-minded men who ran the hospitals were tenacious in defence of their respective institutions. Hospitals were in financial competition with each other, a competition that frequently become bitter when major appeals were made simultaneously, or when the building of a new hospital was contemplated. The outlook was unpromising, and the growing Labour Party believed that, solvent or not, the voluntary system could never adequately meet all the public's needs. The Party's policy was to require local authorities to establish their own hospitals and, as a dual system would create problems, they would then absorb the voluntary hospitals. The medical profession generally opposed this, believing that the state should supplement, not supplant, the voluntary hospitals, and should not deprive them of their independence.

The Victorians entertained the misconception that private charity alone could fill every gap between the very wealthy, who could afford medical treatment, and the destitute workhouse inmate. Suggestions of state assistance were originally met with strong resistance, but the unremitting, intense financial pressures caused cracks to appear in the voluntary system. This spurred its trustees and administrators to cast their nets wider, and after 1919 to consider, and eventually demand, municipal and state subsidies. By 1920, even Viscount Knutsford was suggesting the state should pay one-third of the hospitals' costs. Although the National Health Service did not come into operation until 1948, the voluntary hospitals were on a downward financial path, and, despite their rallying from time to time, it was clear from early in the twentieth century that their days of complete independence were numbered.

The Infirmaries were originally the hospital sections of the Poor Law workhouses, intended solely for their sick inmates. Slowly, over time, they developed into true hospitals and the general public was admitted. They became the first public general hospitals.[7]

Conditions in their wards left much to be desired, and there were frequent cases of ill-treatment. However, attempts were made to improve their staffing and equipment, and London's Poor Law Guardians were increasingly men of vision. By 1909 there was some evidence that the standards of a few of the very best infirmaries were approaching those of the voluntary hospitals.[8] Despite this, there is little doubt that, in general, the service the voluntary hospitals supplied was superior in almost every aspect – in the quality, qualifications and numbers of their medical and nursing staff, and in the equipment and medicine at their disposal. The ratio of staff to patients on 31 March 1901 – in the London Hospital two members of staff to every three patients, in the Whitechapel Infirmary one member of staff to nine patients – tells its own story. Even allowing for the fact that infirmaries admitted more chronic cases requiring less intensive individual attention, this still represented a far superior ratio for the London Hospital. Most infirmaries had operating theatres, but only a few had a bacteriological laboratory or an X-ray department.

The principal East End infirmaries were the Whitechapel Infirmary in Vallance Road (later called St Peter's Hospital and destroyed by bombing in World War II), and the Mile End Infirmary in Bancroft Road (now part of the Royal London Hospital). Though their popularity was growing, they were still indelibly identified in the minds of the sick poor with the workhouses in which families were separated and periods of silence were enforced, even though the infirmaries were by now in separate buildings with their own separate entrances.

They were not at all popular with East End Jews. Reverend A. A. Green, the minister of Hampstead Synagogue, who was born in the East End in 1860 and was actively engaged in East End medical charities, fully understood the thinking of the poor there. He wrote in 1909:[9]

> Much care is bestowed at the infirmary, and great desire exists to do all that is possible for the welfare of the patients. But a workhouse infirmary is a workhouse infirmary when all is said and done ... and the Jew ... is regarded more or less as an alien, and when he can speak only Yiddish this is accentuated. ... It often happens that a Jew who wants to put on his hat when he takes his meals, and who wants to put on tephillin and say his prayers in the morning, is assailed with all manner of blasphemous comment which renders his stay a perfect purgatory.

Reverend W. Esterson, the minister at the Hambro Synagogue, said[10] 'the very name 'infirmary' seems to terrify the East End Jew', and Rev. P. Passenfeld commented[11] that as the cases referred to the infirmaries were of a more chronic and incurable nature than those admitted to the voluntary hospitals, 'the man who is obliged to enter an infirmary feels that his days are numbered, and is therefore more anxious to adhere to his religion than ever'. According to Mr Mark Fineman,[12] an investigator for the Jewish Board of Guardians in the 1920s and 1930s, the taint of the Poor Laws and the fear of being branded as paupers, was a prime cause of the East End Jews' abhorrence of the infirmaries.

Jewish Hospitals

In 1900 there was no Jewish hospital in England, apart from the Beth Holim which was by now restricted mainly to maternity cases. This was surprising given that there had been a tradition of Jewish hospitals since biblical times. There was a Jewish hospital in Cologne in the eleventh century, and one in Munich in the fourteenth. The sixteenth century Jewish hospitals, known as *hekdesh*, served as resting places for those passing through a town, and combined this with rudimentary facilities for medical care. They were usually very primitive, consisting of one or two rooms with a maximum of six beds, ill-equipped for nursing, and without any regular medical attention. They were supported by the local communities, by benevolent societies, and by charity boxes. The reason for the low standards was that most Jewish communities were small, poor, socially insecure and subject to sudden expulsion, so that the provision of permanent facilities for the sick was regarded as a waste of communal resources. With the eighteenth century Enlightenment, and political emancipation, Jewish communities could look forward to a permanent settlement and better economic prospects, and facilities in the *hekdesh* improved.

Gradually, the idea of the modern hospital as we know it today began to take root. In the second half of the eighteenth century Jewish hospitals opened in Berlin, Breslau, and Vienna. The first Jewish hospital in France was founded in Paris in 1836. From then onward Jewish hospitals, with general wards for the poor and private wards for the wealthier classes, were built throughout Europe, and they were to be found in many towns in Lithuania, Latvia, Poland, Romania, Germany and in Salonika in Greece. There was a Jewish hospital in Amsterdam from about 1840, and another in Basle. Italy's first Jewish hospital was established in Rome in 1881. The Jewish hospital in Vienna was built by the Rothschilds. In 1909, there were two Jewish hospitals in Berlin, one supported by the mainstream Jewish community and the other by the more orthodox Adass Yisroel.

In America, German Jewish immigrants who were accustomed to medical care being a Jewish communal function, founded a Jewish hospital in New York in 1852. Originally called Jews' Hospital, it has been known as Mount Sinai Hospital since 1869. The Jewish Hospital of Cincinnati that opened in 1854 additionally provided shelter for the poor and transients during its early years in the traditional manner of the *hekdesh*. After 1900 some of the recently arrived East European immigrants expressed discontent with the 'un-Jewish' atmosphere in the established hospitals, and founded new hospitals in the larger cities. These Jewish hospitals all enjoyed good reputations, and most catered for both Jewish and non-Jewish patients.

London boasted a German Hospital, an Italian Hospital, and a French Hospital. There seemed to be no good reason why there should not also be a Jewish hospital. But it was a curious phenomenon, the cause of which is not easy to pinpoint, that wealthy English Jews who gave impressive support to all manner of Jewish medical charities refused to support a specifically Jewish hospital. Dr. J. Snowman wrote to the *Jewish Chronicle*:[13]

> A tradition has sprung up in Anglo-Jewry that a Jewish hospital is anathema on English soil . . . It is illogical and inconsistent. Though we deprecate a Jewish hospital, we boast of our Home for Incurables. We oppose the establishment of an institution for treating the sick, but we cherish two Homes where our sick may convalesce. We shun the idea of a Jewish hospital, but we eagerly accepted a Sanatorium and justly regard it with pride.

Whatever the reason – (and it most probably stemmed from the way in which English hospitals developed and the close relationship between them and the wealthy Jews of the community) – the beginning of the twentieth century was not a propitious time to establish a new voluntary hospital, Jewish or non-Jewish.

In the absence of a Jewish hospital, the leadership of the London Jewish community made special arrangements for its sick poor by entering into 'understandings' with the voluntary hospitals.

ARRANGEMENTS MADE BY THE JEWISH COMMUNITY WITH LONDON'S VOLUNTARY HOSPITALS

Due to their uneven geographical distribution, voluntary hospitals were available to only a small proportion of England's working population. The immigrant Jews were therefore fortunate that in the midst of the Jewish East End stood the great London Hospital, one of the foremost in the world.

Instituted in 1741, from its earliest days it made arrangements for its Jewish patients to have kosher food. They were given an allowance of $2\frac{1}{2}$ d a day (later increased to 4d and then to 9d) to purchase their own meat and soup, 'but to receive bread and beer like the other patients'. Over the next two hundred years, and indeed until beyond the end of World War II, the London Hospital met requests from the Jewish community for kosher food, Jewish wards, facilities for celebrating the Sabbath and Jewish Festivals, for circumcisions, special visiting hours, and special arrangements for post-mortems. The Hospital even provided separate ice chambers and a mortuary for Jewish bodies, to satisfy the requirements that after death Jewish bodies should be washed according to Talmudic instructions, be attended only by Jews, and to ensure that no organs were removed. The Hospital engaged Jewish almoners, and on the death of a Jewish patient allowed *wachers* into the wards. One of the rules of the Hospital was that out-patients who could afford to do so should pay something towards the cost of medicines or dressings. For the orthodox Jew, carrying money on the Sabbath is forbidden. To overcome this, Jewish members of the House Committee guaranteed to pay for any such Jews who attended on a Sabbath without money.[1]

At any given time there were several Jews on its Board of Governors and House Committee, though there appears to have been 'a Jewish quota' in operation; only as one left was another elected. In 1910, the twenty-five members of the House Committee included Nathaniel Cohen, the Hon. H. L. W. Lawson, Louis Raphael, Alfred Salmon, and A. Stern.

Providing these special facilities obviously involved the Hospital in additional expense. How could the London Hospital afford to be so generous to the Jewish community? The answer lay in the financial support the Hospital received from wealthy Jews. Dr Eardley Holland, a consultant at the Hospital in the 1930s, said[2] that he started his day at the Hospital by lecturing to students in the Bearsted Clinical Theatre; proceeded to operate in a theatre provided by W. B. Levy; conducted pathological researches in the Bernhard Baron Institute; and attended patients in wards named after a Raphael, a Rothschild, and a Stern. At the King Edward VII Hospital Fund, of which he was a commissioner, the Samuel Lewis Bequest was one of the main sources of income. 'In proportion to their numbers, Jewish people give far more to the hospitals in this country than do other persons'.

As early as 1837, the 'Committee for the more effectual relief of the Sick Poor of the Jewish Community requiring medical aid in and about London', *Meshonet Lecholim*, approached the Governors of the London Hospital. They were very keen to have a male and a female ward exclusively for the use of Jewish patients, attended by a male Jewish nurse and a female Jewish nurse respectively, 'by which means the Jewish in-patients would, on their sick and often on their death-beds, receive that consolation and peace of mind which would prove most consonant with their religious feelings'. They also asked for a separate kitchen under the care of a Jewish cook, and for meat to be supplied by a Jewish butcher.

The Committee offered to cover the Hospital's additional costs either by making an annual payment or providing a large capital sum. They left the amount to the Governors, and added:

> As the Governors of the London Hospital are aware, the Jews have been liberal donors to their excellent Charity. The Committee think they are warranted in believing that should the present request be granted, the generosity hitherto displayed by the more opulent of their brethren will be considerably augmented and added to, not alone by them, but by every member of the Jewish community.

In 1842, an agreement was reached by which an annual sum would be paid to the Hospital from a trust fund, the payments to continue 'so long as the said wards are appropriated for the reception of the Jewish patients'.[3] In 1843, a male and a female ward were reserved 'for the comfort of the Hebrew patients'. A letter in the *Jewish Chronicle* in April 1869 from 'A Believing Jew', said that so long as the London Hospital continued to provide as it was doing 'we need not do anything so anti-Jewish as to build a hospital only for Jews'. In 1904, four new Jewish wards were opened in the west wing of the Hospital. Edward Raphael gave £20,000 towards their endowment, and his son, Louis Raphael, contributed generously for their equipment.

Other London hospitals also responded to requests for special provision for their Jewish patients. Two such hospitals close to the East End, and much used by East End Jews, were the German Hospital in Dalston, and the Metropolitan Hospital in Kingsland Road.

The German Hospital was founded in 1845.[4] Its original aim was to cater for poor German emigrants then living and working in the East End of London, largely in the sugar refineries. Many did not speak English, and it was felt they were at a disadvantage in expressing their needs to English doctors and nurses, and in communication with other patients. German clergymen also found it impossible to locate or regularly visit all their parishioners spread around the hospitals of the metropolis. The existence of the German Hospital remedied these deficiencies. Its nursing staff were all recruited from German Protestant deaconesses trained at a special school in Bielefeld.

Because of so many similarities in the languages, it is reasonably easy for German speakers and Yiddish speakers to make themselves understood to each other. At an inaugural meeting held on 18 June 1845, Baron von Bunsen, the Prussian Ambassador in London, who secured the necessary finance for the hospital, said:

> If Jews of the German language present themselves they will, of course, be received like all others, and may be attended by nurses of their own profession. There is to be perfect equality, perfect liberty.

However, in 1894 the Hospital found itself entangled in a religious controversy that was to throw into relief the relationship between itself and the Jewish establishment. Complaints were made that Roman Catholic and Jewish patients, a captive audience, had been compelled to listen to Protestant services held in the wards. Baron Schroder, the Chairman of the Hospital, declared this was perfectly in order as the Hospital was 'a Protestant institution'. The Roman Catholic and Jewish Governors requisitioned a Special General Court of the Governors to consider the matter. At a stormy meeting Louis Davidson, a member of the Council of the United Synagogue and Chairman of its Visiting Committee, said he hoped Baron Schroder would agree that it was unsatisfactory to hold services in the wards, but when Schroder indicated disagreement, Davidson said:

> Baron Schroder shakes his head – I am sorry to see it. I think he would have found it to be in the welfare of the German Hospital. My community do not wish to aggravate matters, we only want fair play for all. If, however, by an unfortunate combination of circumstances, things should not go in the direction we have hoped, then it will not be our fault if subscriptions are withdrawn from the Hospital. But I hope that the Chairman will believe me when I say that we do not put this forward as a threat.

Whatever Davidson's intention, it must have sounded like a threat. Schroder and his committee won a vote of confidence, but it backfired on them; Jewish and Catholic subscribers cancelled or reduced their subscriptions. The Hospital quickly decided it was expedient to change the arrangement, and from then on Roman Catholic and Jewish patients were as far as possible placed in separate wards. The percentage of in-patients who were Jewish rose from 15% in 1894 to 31% in 1907; about 25% of its out-patients were Jewish. It had an East End dispensary in Great Prescott Street, and 'practically every one' of its 2,400 out-patients was Jewish.[5] At its West End dispensary in Great Portland Street the proportion was 75%.

In 1900, the German Hospital authorities agreed to the installation of a kosher kitchen, paid for by a Jewish committee that also made itself responsible for the cost of its maintenance, including the employment of a cook and kitchen maid. The Secretary of the Hospital, in an interview with the *Jewish Chronicle* on 8 March 1907, said:

> In proportion to our size we are doing more for the Jewish community than any other hospital. Of our 130 beds, 40 on an average are occupied by Jews. The Jews come to us because, being a German Hospital, there is no language difficulty. In a small hospital like ours we do not find it practicable to have separate Jewish wards ... but many of our doctors are Jews.

It is easy to understand why the London Hospital was popular with the East End Jews, being in the very heart of the Jewish area and particularly sensitive to Jewish requirements. Similarly, the German Hospital was attractive because of the language spoken by the nurses and doctors. But why the Metropolitan Hospital? Immediately prior to 1894 it had comparatively few Jewish patients. The reason for its subsequent popularity lies in the events that followed the 1894 Governors' Meeting at the German Hospital.

The minutes of the Visitation Committee of the United Synagogue for 23 May 1894 recorded that Davidson had met officials of the Metropolitan who agreed to make special arrangements for the reception of Jewish patients, and to provide a Yiddish-speaking doctor if funds were forthcoming. Davidson said that Messrs Rothschild, Samuel Montagu and others were willing to transfer part of their subscriptions from the German Hospital to the Metropolitan Hospital. A kosher kitchen was installed, and the services of Dr Abraham Cohen,[6] who spoke Yiddish, were obtained. Money began to flow into the Metropolitan's coffers from the Jewish community, and the number of Jewish patients rose. In 1897, 16% of its 1,055 in-patients were Jewish as were 9% of the 100,000 out-patients.

The Metropolitan later provided two Jewish wards. The nurse in charge, Sister Pressland, was described by a patient as knowing 'quite enough to be a *Rebbetzan*'.

Scrupulous regard was paid to dietary and other religious regulations, and the wards were regularly visited by Rev Professor H. Gollancz, the Minister of the Bayswater Synagogue, and several East End ministers. Dr Cohen attended twice a week. The Hospital had many Jewish friends and supporters. Sir George Faudel Phillips, a Governor of Bart's, and Leopold Rothschild were vice-presidents, and Lieut. Colonel Montefiore, Major Sam Wiel, Messrs F. S. Frankel, and D. C. Defries were members of its committee of management. There were numerous Jewish benefactors of the Hospital, including Baroness de Rothschild and Sir Lucien Goldsmid.

The Gentile matron, who clearly had all the attributes required of a good Jewish housewife, was interviewed by the *Jewish Chronicle*:[7]

> I understand all the Jewish traditions, and am very careful about the separation of meat and butter food, and meat and butter utensils. Our patients have their milk puddings half an hour before their meat dinner, as I know that after meat they would have to wait four hours before tasting milk. We have two separate sinks in our kosher kitchen, one for washing up meat things, and another for butter things, and separate cloths also. The Passover utensils are locked away during the year in a cupboard of which I keep the key in my own room. The *seder* dish is most carefully prepared. A student takes the *seder* service, and if he makes any innovations or leaves out anything to which the patients have been accustomed, it is resented. There was much heart-burning one year because the gentleman who gave the *seder* did not make every patient eat the horse radish. Of course, all the Passover food is ordered from a special purveyor. The Friday evening candles are lit by one of our patients or by our Jewish cook. At New Year someone comes to blow the shofar, and on Tabernacles the lulav and esrog are taken round the wards. The muzzuzahs on the doors give great confidence to Jewish patients when they come here.

In November 1909, the Hospital opened two Jewish wards, with thirteen beds, and a separate room for Jewish out-patients. There was also a separate mortuary, with accommodation for *wachers*. Its almoner worked in close co-operation with the Jewish Board of Guardians.

Other London hospitals with Jewish facilities included the Brompton Hospital for Consumption and Diseases of the Chest, at which a Jewish ward was opened in March 1905, together with a kosher kitchen and a special mortuary. This was brought about largely due to the efforts of the Rev L. Geffen, the Jewish visitor, who was supported in this by the Christian chaplain, the Rev H. Hall. By March 1907 there were two Jewish wards, one for males and the other for females. Baron de Hirsch was a generous benefactor. As a result of these special provisions the number of their Jewish subscribers tripled.[8]

Charing Cross Hospital had a ward for Jewish female patients from 1885. Called the Levy Ward, it was endowed by Miss Matilda Levy, the daughter of Joseph Moses Levy the founder of the *Daily Telegraph*. Later a kosher kitchen was built.

The Levy ward was rebuilt and consecrated by Rev S. Singer in 1903 when it was extended from five to twelve beds, all endowed by members of the Levy family. On the wall hung the text, 'The stranger that dwelleth with you shall be as one born among you. And thou shalt love him as thyself'. The Jewish vice-presidents of the hospital in 1907 included Lord Rothschild, Lady Sassoon, Mrs Arnold Gabriel, Mrs Rufus Isaacs, Solomon Joel, Assur Keyser, Miss Matilda Levy, Mrs Stuart Samuel, Mrs Sylvester Samuel, Mrs Meyer Spielman, and Sir Edward Stern.

The Medical Missions

Christian organisations that sought to convert Jews were active in the East End from the beginning of the nineteenth century, opening free schools in the Jewish area; but it was their medical missions that were to cause the Jewish community its greatest heartache. They began to open shortly after the Jewish Board of Guardians ended its medical department in 1879 and made no secret of their objective. The *East End Mission* said:[9]

> The sole aim of our medical work is to lead these people from Judaism to the light of the Gospel, and to heal the disease of the soul through curing the sickness of the body. Hundreds owe their conversion to the Providence which, working through their sickness, brought them to the Medical Mission.

The London Society for Promoting Christianity among the Jews acquired premises at 4 Goulstone Street in 1891 for what was described as 'aggressive evangelistic work'. In his history of the Society,[10] Reverend W. T. Gidney wrote:

> With thousands of Jews on every hand, it was admirably suited for this purpose, being in the midst of the dense and poor Jewish population of the East End, chiefly hailing from Russia and speaking Yiddish. The combination of a medical missionary organisation, with efforts of a more direct spiritual character, has tended to make the work very effective and telling.

At different times during the period 1880–1939, there were at least nine medical missions in the Jewish East End, including missions in Fournier Street, Whitechapel Road, Cambridge Road, Commercial Road, Buxton Street and Philpot Street. For most East End Jews a medical mission was just around the corner. According to a letter in the *Jewish Chronicle*, all those who attended 'had first to hear a lengthy sermon preached against our religion, which is held to ridicule and to which they listen in silence, afraid to say a word for fear of not being able to see the doctor'.[11]

Every morning at about 8.30 a.m., and every afternoon at about 1 o'clock, there was a large crowd, 99% of whom were Jewish, outside Philpot Street mission hall.

The doors were sometimes locked from the inside so that it was impossible to escape the prayers. Its staff consisted of two full-time doctors, two part-time doctors, one dentist, one consulting dentist, three lady dispensers, and three assistants. A Yiddish-speaking nurse was always available. It was open every day of the week until 3 p.m. and a number of patients were allowed to recuperate at the Mission's Convalescent Home at Brentwood in Essex.

The Mildmay Mission Hospital in Austin Street, Shoreditch did not have the conversion of Jews to Christianity as its main purpose; Jews were accepted rather than sought. It was an evangelical institution, run on strictly Christian lines, with frequent services for the patients and biblical texts adorning the walls. Founded in 1866, it initially had little more than the occasional Jewish patient, but pronounced itself 'glad to have the opportunity of showing kindness to the seed of Abraham'. From the turn of the twentieth century the numbers increased. 'Many of them could not speak English, but the same loving service in the same Christian spirit was shown to Jew and Gentile alike. The confidence of these people was soon won'.[12] Its 1904 Annual Report noted yet a further increase, and claimed that some 'had received the Gospel'.

The missions were undoubtedly popular. Many East End Jews could not afford the local 'sixpenny doctor'; resented the long waiting time, (up to seven hours), in the hospital out-patient departments; and were unhappy at the thought of undergoing a searching and sometimes unpleasant inquiry from a parochial Receiving Officer. Mission doctors won their confidence and enjoyed a reputation for skill. They did not hurry the patient, and allowed time for general conversation and sympathy. 'There is such a thing as curing by sympathy', a witness told the United Synagogue's 1912 Enquiry into the Missions. Importantly, they were an additional source of treatment. Another witness told the Enquiry that if a fresh batch of doctors came into the East End they would all find work, and none of the existing doctors would suffer; the Jews would consult both.

East End Jews had few qualms about availing themselves of missionary medical care – they took the leaflets, listened to the prayers and sermons (although some women, squalling children in their arms, stuffed their ears with cotton wool so that they should not hear the name of Christ), and departed none the worse for wear. The medical missions were a valuable additional source of medical care for the Jewish poor, and the evidence reveals that there were very few true converts.

The efforts of the wealthier elements in the community to provide adequate hospital care for London's Jewish poor had paid excellent dividends. But there were some, including Berliner and his friends, who were not fully satisfied with what was on offer.

MANCHESTER VICTORIA MEMORIAL JEWISH HOSPITAL

It used to be said, by Mancunians, that what Manchester does today London does tomorrow. This was certainly true of the Jewish Hospital, because there was a trial run there; and the Manchester experience provided an insight for those who later fought to establish a Jewish Hospital in London.

In one vital aspect the situation in Manchester was completely different from London where, as has been seen, there were several hospitals and infirmaries catering for Jewish religious requirements. None such existed in Manchester. Further, the Manchester Jewish elite was not so deeply entrenched in the voluntary hospital movement as were the London community leaders.

In 1900, the Jewish population of Manchester was between 20,000 and 25,000, divided, as in London, between the established community and the new immigrants. On 3 August 1900, the *Jewish Chronicle* reported that a meeting had been held to discuss a proposal for founding a Jewish hospital. It was estimated that only £1,000 was needed to buy and convert a suitable house, and £20 to £30 a week to maintain it.

The recent immigrant poor immediately welcomed the scheme warmly, as did local Jewish general practitioners. Those in favour argued that some Jews who should enter hospital did not do so because their religious principles would be compromised, particularly in the absence of kosher food. Further, it was said, hospitals were so overcrowded and congested that any additional facilities would help to relieve the pressure on them. On the other side it was contended, and this was to be one of the main arguments later developed, that Jews should not segregate themselves from the general population; rather they should assimilate and enjoy together the facilities already freely available to all, regardless of creed. An important and influential opponent was Nathan Laski, president of the Manchester Old Hebrew Congregation, who declared that such a hospital was quite unnecessary.

A second 'well-attended' meeting took place on 7 September 1900. Great interest had been excited locally, and both opponents and supporters were present. The original arguments were expanded and fresh ones raised. It was said that a

Jewish hospital was needed because the *mitzvah*, the duty, of visiting the sick, *Bikkur Cholim*, was not carried out in England as conscientiously as it was on the Continent, and the hospital would help fill that gap. Another point raised was that many Jewish patients could not speak English at all, which caused problems of communication that led to misunderstanding by doctors of the patients' complaints and needs. Further, such a hospital, it was said, would provide facilities for the training of Jewish nurses of whom there was a dearth. It was also claimed that the presence of a Jewish hospital would promote better hygienic conditions and awareness among the Jewish community at large.

Against this it was contended that it would be sufficient if kosher kitchens were provided in local hospitals. Existing hospitals were desperately short of funds and Jews should give their money to them rather than spend it on a new institution.

A resolution was carried, 'almost unanimously', that the time had arrived to establish a Jewish Hospital in Manchester, and a large number of those present completed forms of subscription, and promised active support for the hospital. Dr Charles Dreyfus J.P., a Conservative city councillor and prominent Zionist, was appointed chairman of the Appeal Committee and became the effective leader of the movement.

The first correspondence appeared in the *Jewish Chronicle* of 14 September 1900, under the heading 'A Jewish Hospital – Is it needed?' Reverend Simeon Singer, the Minister of London's New West End Synagogue and a former headmaster of Jews' College, wrote:

Sir – The movement ... is calculated to arouse in many earnest Jews feelings of alarm and regret ... the formation of a sectarian hospital is absolutely unnecessary. Our hospitals concern themselves solely with the need, not the creed, of the sufferers who seek their aid ... the establishment of a distinctively Jewish hospital will, I fear, expose us to a very serious charge – 'What strange people these Jews are', our neighbours will say of us. 'We do not exclude them, nor do we dream of excluding them from our hospitals. Yet even so they are not content. They must exclude themselves'. ... The language difficulty is to a great extent exaggerated. In practice it solves itself fairly easily. The necessities of the patients on one hand, and the goodwill of the doctors and the nurses on the other, soon establish a working understanding between them. The very difficulty provides an additional inducement for our foreign brethren to learn the language of the country where they are hospitably received ... It is hardly possible to overrate the privilege we all enjoy in this country of an undenominational hospital system. May we Jews, on our part, also continue to be guided by the principle that 'as there is no sectarianism in misery so should there be none in mercy'.

This introduced emotive language into the argument. The movement would 'cause alarm'; Jews would be 'exposed to a serious charge'; non-Jews would 'think Jews strange'. The profession of the author was also significant in that, with few exceptions, the ministry were against the idea of a Jewish Hospital. It was not surprising that Reverend Singer was opposed. He was the English translator of the Authorised Daily Prayer Book used by the United Hebrew Congregations. It was subsidised by Mrs Nathaniel Montefiore so that it could sell for one shilling, and one purpose of this was to help the new immigrants to anglicize themselves. Anything likely to run counter to this was likely to be opposed by those who considered integration imperative.

'Layman of Manchester' put another point that clearly exercised the minds of the opponents. He claimed that there was a danger that they might create a Jewish hospital ghetto. He warned that all Jewish cases, no matter from which district, would be referred to the Jewish hospital, and so in time the Jews would exclude themselves from the benefits of the public hospitals, 'a calamity and a danger to the well-being of our poor brethren, who, should the Jewish Hospital collapse from a lack of financial support, would later on have to beg for the re-opening of those channels of medical assistance which are now freely accorded to all, irrespective of creed or race'.

It was also said that other hospital charities would rightly fear that funds would be diverted away from them. Although it was to be some time before this fear was to be openly expressed by the hospital authorities, the move for a Jewish hospital in Manchester must have been followed with interest, and some concern, by the great general voluntary hospitals of London, particularly the East End hospitals, and even more particularly by the London Hospital.

Dr Berendt Salomon, Minister of the Manchester Old Hebrew Congregation, described as 'the chief Jewish minister in the City', said in an interview with the *Jewish World*,[1] that the scheme bordered on the impossible. The charity burden on the Jewish community was already great enough, and the movement could succeed only if, as on the Continent, it was fully endowed by a philanthropist. He warned that the penny contributions from the poor could be affected by strikes, or depression in trade, and said he had received support for his views from the Chief Rabbi, Hermann Adler. 'Why', he was asked, 'are there so many Jewish hospitals on the Continent?' 'Because', said Salomon, 'there no Jew, unless he is a native, and then only with the utmost difficulty, is admitted into municipal institutions, and so is compelled to have recourse to his own. Such arrangements are not needed in enlightened England'.

An approach was made to the Manchester Royal Infirmary to ascertain whether it was prepared to provide a kosher kitchen for Jewish patients. The reply was that it did not have sufficient space.

At the end of October, there was a further conference at Derby Hall, at which 'sober, earnest, and thoughtful' discussion took place.[2] It was said that in a sympathetic Jewish environment the Jewish sick would heal faster, and the burden on the Jewish Board of Guardians would be lessened. The Haham, Dr. Moses Gaster, the religious leader of the Sephardi community of England, was later to embroider the point when he said[3] that religious scruples connected with food, custom and language made it difficult for a Jew to receive treatment in a public hospital. 'Are we justified', he asked rhetorically, 'in adding one atom of spiritual agony to the physical suffering of the conscientious and religious Jew? If we can for one moment relieve him from that terrible anguish of mind, we will do more to help him than all the medical assistance we can possibly render'.

Joseph Dulberg, a local general practitioner, agreed:[4]

Speaking from experience, the chief reason why the poor, uneducated Jews refuse, or at least hesitate, to enter a general hospital not only here in England, but elsewhere too, is the ... presentiment that the absence of Jewish sympathy and Jewish ministration will bring about death instead of a cure.

Until this point the *Jewish Chronicle* had contented itself with reporting the arguments and the progress of the scheme, but on 30 November 1900 it expressed its own opinion. A Jewish hospital, it pronounced, was unnecessary. It was sufficient to use the community's energy and money to obtain Jewish wards and kosher kitchens in existing hospitals. Besides, 'admission of Jews into an undenominational hospital ensures the co-operation of Jews and Christians in the support of the medical charities'.

The *Jewish Chronicle* was nearly sixty years old, and was the strongest voice in the Jewish press. Its opposition must have saddened the promoters of the scheme and encouraged its opponents. To make matters worse, the Manchester Royal Infirmary announced a change of mind, and said it would agree to having kosher food brought in for an experimental period of twelve months – at the expense of the Jewish community. This effectively scuppered an important part of the promoters' argument, but despite all the opposition, they intimated in a quiet but firm manner that nothing would deter them from persevering with their project. The cost of a hospital of twenty beds, now their aim, would be £6,000.

On 14 March 1902, the *Jewish Chronicle* surprisingly reported that the agitation could be coming to an end. The Manchester Royal Infirmary was planning to move to Stanley Grove, three miles from the Jewish neighbourhood, and was considering including a Jewish ward or wards in the new building. 'Should this be the case', the *Jewish Chronicle* commented, 'a knotty question will have been satisfactorily solved which at one time seriously threatened the disruption of the good relations between class and class'. In the meantime, it hoped that the committee of the proposed hospital would stay their hand, and not commit themselves to a position from which it might be difficult afterwards to recede. This report showed clearly how the Jewish hospital argument had divided the Manchester community on class lines – the poorer section of the community in favour of having a Jewish hospital, and the wealthy against. The Infirmary's offer was later declined, principally because it was considered that the new site was too far from Cheetham where a large proportion of Manchester Jews lived.

On 15 May 1903, the Jewish Hospital Committee announced that the purchase of a site had been completed, and building operations commenced. They claimed that opposition to the scheme had practically disappeared, and expressed the hope that those who had hitherto held aloof would follow the example of the Chief Rabbi and the Rev B. Salomon who had now signified their support by contributing to the funds.

The Manchester Victoria Memorial Jewish Hospital, at the junction of Elizabeth Street and Sherbourne Street, Cheetham Park, opened on Thursday, 17 November 1904, just a little more than three years after the start of the campaign. The Chief Rabbi was not present, but in the light of subsequent events it was significant that the Haham was. The building was of red brick, two storeys high. There were two wards with ten beds each on the first floor, and one four-bed and one six-bed ward on the ground floor. The Haham said that many who had withheld support had since been drawn to the hospital with newly awakened feelings of deep sympathy. 'Many who doubted have seen their doubts melt away in the light of the rising sun'.[5]

Contributions from the poor were running at £400 per annum, and N. M. Rothschild & Sons made a handsome donation. Bernard Kostoris gave five hundred guineas, and Jacob Moser of Bradford gave £250 and promised to furnish two wards.[6]

The ground had been laid for a similar movement in London. Would the course of events be the same there?

JEWISH COMMUNITY CARE FOR ITS SICK POOR BEFORE 1880

[1] *Jewish Chronicle*, 18 March 1912.

[2] *The Sephardim of England* (1951), Albert Hymanson, pp. 40, 49, 59, 82.

[3] For details of the work of the Board see Lipman V. D., *A Century of Social Service 1859–1959* (1959), and Gerry Black, unpublished Ph.D. thesis, *Health and Medical Care of the Jewish Poor in the East End of London 1880–1939*. Leicester University, 1987. A copy of the thesis is at Tower Hamlets Local History Library, Bancroft Road.

[4] *The Jewish Board of Guardians Annual Report 1863*. Appendix B.

[5] *Royal Commission on the Poor Laws*, 1909. Cd. 4499. Evidence, question 41,888 and 41,921–3.

[6] *Annual Report* for 1879, p. 26.

[7] For additional information see Lara Marks. *Dear Old Mother Levy's: the Jewish Maternity Home and Sick Rooms Society 1895–1939*, published 1990 by The Society for the Social History of Medicine.

[8] The home became known as 'Mrs Levy's', named after its long serving superintendent. In 1938, it moved to a new site, in Lordship Road, Stoke Newington, under the name of The Bearsted Memorial Hospital. It has since closed.

[9] In an article in the *Jewish Chronicle* in May 1926.

THE VOLUNTARY HOSPITALS AND THE INFIRMARIES

[1] In letter of 28 June 1924, Viscount Knutsford to Guardians of Parish of Fulham. In the London Hospital archives.

[2] In an address to the Labour Party Conference at Caxton Hall in April 1924.

[3] For more detailed discussion of the history of the hospitals see *The Hospitals 1800–1948*, Brian Abel-Smith (1964) and *The Development of the London Hospital System 1832–1982*, Geoffrey Rivett (1986).

[4] Sir Henry Burdett, speaking at annual meeting of House Hospital Association, 17 March 1910. And see Rivett pp. 28, 29; *Encyclopaedia Britannica* 11th Ed 1911.

[5] *Encyclopaedia Britannica* 11th Edition, 1911/12.

[6] In 1920 the King Edward Fund distributed £700,000, the Sunday Fund £110,000, and the Saturday Fund, £73,000.

[7] See *The Origins of the National Health Service* (1967), Ruth Hodgkinson pp. 451+.

[8] See Royal Commission on the Poor Laws, 1909.

[9] *Jewish Chronicle* 1 January 1909.

[10] *Jewish Chronicle* 2 May 1909.

[11] *Jewish Chronicle* 8 June 1923.

[12] In an interview with the author.

[13] 5 February 1909.

ARRANGEMENTS MADE BY THE JEWISH COMMUNITY WITH LONDON'S VOLUNTARY HOSPITALS

[1] See E. W. Morris, *A History of the London Hospital*, (1926).

[2] *Jewish Chronicle* 9 July 1937.

[3] The income from the trust, later known as the Rothschild Fund, was still being paid to the Hospital well after the end of World War II.

[4] For a full history of the German Hospital see *An Account of the German Hospital in London 1845–1948*, PhD thesis by Mrs M. Neuman 1969. Copy at St Bartholomew's Hospital archives.

[5] *Jewish Chronicle* 8 March 1907.

[6] He had been Resident Physician at the Royal United Hospitals in Bath and for many years was honorary medical officer to the Jewish Convalescent homes at Brighton and Norwood.

[7] 8 March 1907.

[8] *Jewish Chronicle*, 8 March 1907.

[9] Quoted in the *United Synagogue Mission Committee Report of 1912*.

[10] *The History of the London Society for Promoting Christianity Among the Jews 1809–1908*. At p. 533.

[11] *Jewish Chronicle* 12 December 1913.

[12] *The Mildmay Mission Hospital. The Second Mile*. Pamphlet, London (1943)

MANCHESTER VICTORIA MEMORIAL JEWISH HOSPITAL

[1] 9 November 1900.

[2] *Jewish World* 2 November 1900.

[3] *Jewish World* 31 July 1903.

[4] *Jewish Chronicle* 14 September 1900.

[5] *Jewish World* 18 November 1904.

[6] There was also a small hospital in Leeds, originally called the Herzl-Moser Home of the Jewish Sick, and later renamed the Herzl-Moser Hospital. It was largely dependent on Jacob Moser's philanthropy. By 1911 it had twelve beds.

The Struggle

THE CAST

There were five principal protagonists in the London controversy. Nathaniel Meyer, the first Lord Rothschild [1840–1915], popularly known as 'Natty', was the eldest son of Baron Lionel de Rothschild. The Rothschild family had advanced the welfare of the Jews to a far greater extent than any other, and Natty was perhaps the most generous of them all. Born in Piccadilly, he had his barmitzvah at the Great Synagogue, Duke's Place on 19 November 1853. After attending Trinity College, Cambridge, where he formed an enduring friendship with the Prince of Wales, later Edward VII, he took a position at New Court in the family banking house. There he retained the tradition that no business was transacted on Saturdays. He married Emma, the daughter of Baron Charles de Rothschild of Frankfurt, and they had homes at 148 Piccadilly, at Gunnersbury Park, and at Tring. After his father's death in 1879 he became head of the firm, and in 1885 became the first Jewish peer. From that time, as Chaim Bermant has observed,[1] 'when Jews consoled themselves with the expression 'the Lord will provide' they usually meant Lord Rothschild'.

On his Tring estate he provided free medical treatment, free nursing, free housing, and old age pensions for his employees and tenants. He was elected to high office in many of Anglo-Jewry's institutions, and worked actively in them. Among many other posts, he was President of the United Synagogue and of the Jews' Free School; Honorary President of the Federation of Synagogues; and Chairman and moving spirit of the Four Percent Industrial Dwellings Company. He was a substantial contributor to the funds of the Russo-Jewish Committee and the Poor Jews' Temporary Shelter, and his name headed the list of almost every charitable appeal.

He took a particularly keen interest in the welfare of the sick poor, and was associated with the work of a number of voluntary hospitals. As Treasurer of the King Edward VII Hospital Fund from its foundation, he was close to Viscount Knutsford who joined the Fund's executive committee in 1909. Like Knutsford, he was especially interested in promoting uniform, economic, and efficient administration in hospitals. He held strong views on this, and in particular set his face steadily against what he conceived to be unnecessary new institutions and the multiplication of charities with the same object.

Many of the concessions the Jewish community had won from the hospital service, particularly from the London Hospital, were the result of his efforts. He was anxious not to jeopardise them by the creation of a specifically Jewish hospital which he feared might diminish Jewish support for the older charities. Although proudly Jewish, he believed Jews should accept the traditions of the country in which they found themselves and harmonise with them, rather than separate themselves from them.

Gifted with a vivid imagination, and able to take a world view of events, his advice was frequently sought by the British government. He was the undoubted lay leader of the English Jewish community; a community that was in awe of his wealth, his international reputation, and his legendary philanthropy. For many, particularly for the wealthier section, his word was law.

It was said that there was a touch of greatness about him, that he was the supreme example of a genius taking pains. He was thorough, keen on detail, and whatever he put his hand to was carried out with all his might. He set his mind and influence against the establishment of a Jewish hospital in London. It would need a bold, brave, perhaps naïve, or foolhardy, opponent to take him on.

Sir Sydney George Holland, 3rd Baronet and 2nd Viscount Knutsford, was born in London on 18 March 1855, the elder of twin sons of the first Viscount Knutsford. He was educated at Wellington and Trinity Hall, Cambridge, and was called to the bar in 1879. After moderate success in his career, he became a director of the East and West India Dock Co. and led for the employers' side during the dock strike of 1889. His contact with the dock labourers, who acknowledged his fairness in the dispute and recognised his genuine sense of sympathy, led him to visit them at Poplar Hospital which received most of the dock accident cases, and he became a governor there in 1891. A great motivator, he caught the imagination, and inspired the enthusiasm, of staff and students, of doctors and nurses, of lay workers, of cleaners, of all and sundry. The Poplar Hospital was then in a parlous financial state, but he speedily remedied its fortunes. Within four years he had raised enough money to make it one of the best smaller hospitals in London. In 1896, he applied to join the House Committee of the London Hospital. He was accepted, and within a year was Chairman, a position he held for thirty-five years until his death, in the Hospital, in 1931.

Known as 'The Prince of Beggars', or in Jewish circles as 'The Prince of Schnorrers', he raised more than five million pounds for his beloved 'London'. Publicity was his first weapon. Although no sentimentalist, he knew how to play on the emotions. A great showman, he 'raised money out of laughter and conjured up cheques out of tears'.[2] If he thought a cheque too small, he would tear it up and send back the bits, demanding more; and usually he got it. Basil Henriques said of him,[3] 'he may have been unscrupulous in the way that he got money for the Hospital, but he was so delightful about it that one forgave him completely'. He set about making 'The London', the greatest hospital in the country.

To achieve this, he steamrollered all opposition, and ruled his Governors with a rod of iron. He dominated meetings of the House Committee which normally approved decisions he had already made. Time spent talking was cut to the minimum, and kept strictly to policy. Increasingly deaf in his later years, he ostentatiously switched off his large hearing box (specially made for him) if anyone was courageous enough to disagree.[4] He lacked neither ability nor modesty, and dedicated his autobiography to 'the man I have known longest and loved most, myself'.[5] A great organiser, he could undoubtedly be counted among the founders of modern hospital efficiency. He was a good friend of Rothschild, whose family had been supporters of the London Hospital since before the days of Waterloo. Together, Rothschild and Viscount Knutsford made a seemingly impregnable partnership.

Whereas Viscount Knutsford loved the good things in life, and spent his spare time and money on the grouse moors, it is doubtful whether Isador Berliner had ever seen a grouse, let alone a grouse moor. He was born on 1 April 1871 in the Province of Petrokov Gourbercy, Russia, the son of Shyer and Rose Berliner. He was already married when he came to England in 1891, and by the time he applied for naturalisation in 1903 had three children, and lived and worked as a barber at 163 Cannon Street Road in the East End. There was more to him than met the eye, for despite this apparently humble and unimportant status he clearly had leadership qualities. He was President of the successful and fairly wealthy Cracow Jewish Friendly Society (founded in 1866) whose members presented him with a gold hunter watch and a photographic portrait in recognition of his services to them.

It was noted on his Home Office naturalisation file that until 1901 he had been active and very much in sympathy with the Polish revolutionary movement in the East End, and though he seldom attended their meetings, was reported to have given them financial support. The police officer who investigated his background on behalf of the Home Office wrote: 'Within the past two years Berliner has, I am informed, kept himself aloof from the revolutionary movements, and intends to remain permanently in the City of London and enjoy the privileges of a British subject'. An official noted, 'Nothing against him except a desire to promote revolution in Poland. Has now quietened down'. His application was granted.

Strictly orthodox, and a prominent member of the Hambro Synagogue in Adler Street, (then called Union Street), Berliner became a patient in the Whitechapel

Infirmary in about 1905. Because he attached great store by his Jewish ritual practices, he found that he suffered more distress and discomfort from this non-Jewish environment than he did from his illness, and realised that the same would apply to others of similar beliefs. Neither the kind attention and patience of the nurses, nor the skill of the doctors, could overcome the real anxiety constantly felt by the totally observant Jew who became a hospital patient, particularly the foreign Jew. He had also attended the Goulston Street Medical Mission shortly after he arrived in London, and was aware of the dangers the missionaries posed.[6] Berliner resolved to spend all his spare time in attempting to found a Jewish hospital in London. For an East End barber, this was indeed to indulge in a dream.

His main allies were to prove to be the local general practitioners and the Jewish poor of the East End, the latter mainly employed in humble positions in the immigrant trades, with earnings of two pounds a week or less. He urgently needed support from a heavyweight establishment figure, and eventually found him in the person of the Haham, Dr Moses Gaster [1856–1939]. Gaster was born in Bucharest, the son of a Dutch diplomatic agent, and his family were the acknowledged lay leaders of the Bucharest Jewish community. Extremely learned and intellectually gifted, he was educated at Bucharest and Leipzig Universities. In addition to his rabbinical studies he had a great interest in philology, and obtained his doctorate with a thesis on the changes of the letter 'e' in the Romanian language, which, if nothing else, indicated he was a man gifted with the ability to concentrate on a subject. After a most successful academic career, he came into conflict with the Romanian government over the issue of Jewish emancipation, and was expelled in 1885. He came to England and, following one particularly brilliant lecture, was offered, and accepted, the post of Haham to the Sephardi community, notwithstanding his Ashkenazi birth.

He was not a man accustomed, or fitted by temperament, to play a minor role. Tact was not his forte. Of great strength of character, he had the defects of his qualities. His intellectual eminence led to intolerance at times; his vanity was easily wounded, and his sense of personal dignity could be readily inflamed, which led him to waste his energies on personal petty quarrels. One of the fathers of political Zionism in Great Britain, he fought almost everybody in the movement at one time or another, including Herzl.

In his mind he was never wrong, and expressed his opinions on a variety of subjects with vehemence, and could 'thunder at his opponents with the majestic wrath of a Hebrew prophet'.[7] Not always submissive to criticism, no matter from which quarter it came, he was a personality no one could overlook. Ever watchful over the interests of the Jewish immigrant community, and particularly sympathetic to them because he was an immigrant himself, he strongly identified with their desires. It may well be that if such desires were opposed by the Jewish establishment that would by itself be enough to ensure his support. If Lord Rothschild and Viscount Knutsford were to be against you, you could do no better than to have Gaster with you.

Another prominent, and possibly decisive, participant was Leopold Jacob Greenberg [1861–1931] who took control of the *Jewish Chronicle* in January 1907, and was its editor until his death. Inflexible in pursuit of what he believed right, he was a man of absolute integrity and strong convictions. He left a mark on Anglo-Jewish journalism more profound than any of his predecessors, and made the *Jewish Chronicle* a force in the country as well as in Jewish circles. Under his leadership the journal progressed from being a mirror of Anglo-Jewish opinion to becoming an active player in historical events.

Born in Birmingham, with a journalistic and Zionist background, a main object for his acquiring the *Jewish Chronicle* was to use its columns to further the Zionist cause.[8] He favoured unrestricted immigration, and threw himself heart and soul into the defence of poor Russian Jewish refugees, and was an impressive witness before the Royal Commission on Alien Immigration.

In its obituary of him, the *Jewish Chronicle* said:[9]

> The possession of wealth and rank weighed as nothing when he came to judge, or rather to appraise, his fellow man. Only in one respect did he differentiate between the wealthy and the poor, the famous and the insignificant. For those to whom power and riches had been granted, he demanded an appreciation of the responsibility which was theirs. And the misdeeds of the great he ever regarded as betrayal as well as wrong.

Communal leaders were castigated by him with the utmost fearlessness if he thought it appropriate. He could be generous to those whose causes aroused his support, but was capable of being vituperative, sarcastic, and savagely critical of those whose policies he opposed.

Rothschild, Knutsford, Berliner, Gaster and Greenberg were the personalities who became most prominent in the public eye, but as events unfolded further figures emerged who were to play highly significant roles in shouldering the burden of the day-to-day, grinding, practical work during the movement's early difficult days.

An intriguing, and unlikely ally of Berliner, was Dr Alfred Goodman Levy [1866–1954], M.D., M.R.C.S., L.R.C.P., as different from Berliner as is possible to imagine. Austere, more English than the English, a dedicated fly-fishing man, and a pioneer in colour photography, he was completely non-orthodox. Born in

Melbourne, where his middle class English-born parents had emigrated, and where his father was involved in the import trade, he was still young when the family returned to England. He was educated at University College School and received his medical training at University College Hospital. His first position was assistant resident medical officer to the Stamford Hill, Stoke Newington, Clapton and Kingsland Dispensary. At the age of twenty-eight he joined the British South Africa Company as district surgeon of Bulawayo, (its first doctor), and spent two years there in charge of its small hospital. A keen surgeon, he became very popular with his patients, and when he was barred from working at the hospital due to a disagreement with officials over his carrying on a private practice at the same time, a petition was signed by 575 of the local residents, and he was immediately reinstated. On his return to England in 1896 he took up research work at University College Hospital School, and became resident anaesthetist at Guy's Hospital.

He married Mary Louisa Isaac, the daughter of Frederick Simeon Isaac, a wealthy man with business interests in South America. The couple lived in a fine house at 2 Manchester Square where Goodman Levy had consulting rooms. Their four children spent much of their time in upper floors reserved for them and their nanny.

His wife, in contrast to her husband, was warm, religiously inclined, an accomplished violinist, a linguist, a keen Zionist, an idealist heavily engaged in charitable work. She went round collecting for the poor of the East End, and counted Lily Montagu and other prominent social workers amongst her friends. Some of her enthusiasm seems to have rubbed off on her husband.

In October 1908, Goodman Levy and Dr Leopold Mandel, who later also played an important part in the Hospital's development, were present at one of the London Jewish Hospital Association's public meetings, having gone with the firm intention of expressing their opposition. Instead, they became converts. Goodman Levy wrote to its secretary, Nathan Jacobowicz, who provided him with details of their membership and aspirations,[10] and from that moment on Goodman Levy became a leading figure in the movement.

Dr Anghel Gaster M.B. [1863–1930] was the younger brother of the Haham. Well qualified medically, both in his native Hungary and in England, he worked at the City of London Hospital for Diseases of the Chest; at Kensington and Fulham General Hospital; and during World War I acted as Commanding Officer of the Military Hospital in Hampstead. For more than thirty years he was medical officer to the Baroness de Hirsch Convalescent Home, also in Hampstead. He was deeply devoted to the welfare of poor East End Jews, and was ever ready to serve them in any way he could. In October 1907, he sent a letter to be read at the first meeting of the Central Committee of the proposed Jewish hospital pledging his support, which, said the *Jewish Chronicle*, 'coming from so authoritative a source cannot but act as a stimulant to further activity'. An outstanding personality and excellent orator, his clarity of mind and speech proved to be a telling influence. When the outlook was grim, as it frequently was, his enthusiasm encouraged the other members of the Committee to continue their struggle.

Dr Leopold Leibster [1868–1932] was the foremost local general practitioner to give Berliner early support. Born in Lublin, Poland he came to England at the turn of the century and built up a large practice at 77 Commercial Street, and attended upon Theodore Herzl when he was in London. An ardent worker for good causes, he and his wife Augusta were heavily engaged in the movement's public meetings.

Mrs L. A. Levy, whose eloquent speeches in both English and Yiddish played an important part in rousing the movement's supporters, was a pioneer of the Women's Zionist movement. She had been active in communal work for over thirty years, having started with district visiting on behalf of Lady Goldsmid, Baroness de Rothschild, Mrs Nathaniel Montefiore, and Mrs Lionel Lucas. She worked for the Jewish Board of Guardians, and was one of the earliest members of its Visitation Committee. Her fluent command of Yiddish and German was invaluable for her work among the Jewish poor in the East End. She had been a patient at the London Hospital in about 1880 and well understood the plight of the sick poor Jew who could not speak English. Ever since that time she had harboured in her mind the idea of a Jewish hospital in London, and when approached by some of Berliner's colleagues was able to tell them, truthfully, that the establishment of a Jewish hospital had been a long standing ambition of hers, and that she was only too willing to help. She proved herself to be an influential and experienced addition to the team.

With such a cast, and such a plot, it was inevitable that a strong drama would unfold.

THE EARLY DAYS

Berliner and his friends held their first public meeting on Sunday, 10 February 1907, at Cannon Street Road Synagogue. The *Jewish Chronicle* reported[1] that the meeting was most enthusiastic, and that the majority of those present joined the movement. A resolution was passed to establish a Jewish hospital in the East End.

It was agreed that subscriptions would range from one penny a week, and to save expense Committee members would act as collectors. Particular emphasis was placed on the need to combat the 'crying evil' of the activities of the missionaries at the Philpot Street Mission and other conversionist centres, and it was argued that the establishment of a Jewish hospital for in-patients as well as out-patients would nullify these efforts. The *Jewish Chronicle* reporter added:

> Considering the poorness of the locality, the financial results accruing from the gathering was particularly gratifying. One working man donated a sovereign, and his practical support encouraged others to hand over their mite. The majority of the members are Zionists. There has long been a feeling that an institution of this nature was much to be desired. The progress of the scheme will be awaited with great interest.

However, there was an immediate and crushing editorial rejoinder in the very next issue of the *Jewish Chronicle* that did not at all reflect the sympathetic report of the week before. 'In the interests of the Jewish community and the Jewish poor', it said, 'we trust that the Committee ... will pause to consider the immense difficulties and disadvantages with which they are faced'.

The paper declared its admiration for the working man who donated a sovereign, but had the Committee calculated how many sovereigns would be needed to found a hospital, and how many to maintain it? Even if they could raise the funds, was a Jewish hospital needed in the East End, and would it have any chance of successfully competing with the larger hospitals already in existence? The answer to each of these questions, it said, was 'no', since every provision for the sick poor, including provision for their religious requirements, was already made in the London Hospital and the Metropolitan Hospital to name but two. Existing hospitals had up-to-date facilities that the new Committee could not provide unless a multi-millionaire came to their support. Further, a denominational hospital would also be at a disadvantage from the outset, because it would not have the support of sources of revenue like the Hospital Sunday Fund that gave money only to the general hospitals. As for the conversionist argument, the *Jewish Chronicle* said, that carried no weight. The same argument had been used in relation to the Jewish Provident Dispensary that had opened in Leman Street in 1900, and that had ended in failure. The major hospitals made special provision for Jewish out-patients, yet many Jews still went to the missionary dispensaries, proving that some preferred missions to hospitals; the existence of a Jewish hospital would not change their ways.

Despite this setback, the Committee continued their work. At a further public meeting on 1 March, speakers were careful to emphasise they were in no way antagonistic to the existing hospitals, but intended to supplement them, and pointed to the shortage of hospital beds in London, only two beds for every 1,000 inhabitants.[2] They said they did not imagine their pennies would produce a hospital to vie with the existing hospitals, but intended to start in a very small way, and would be more than satisfied with three small wards, with fourteen beds.

The *Jewish Chronicle* reported[3] that, as it had anticipated, 'the community' frowned upon the scheme, and that some of the most earnest East End workers, such as Reverend J. F. Stern of the East End Synagogue, had pronounced against it. It is not quite clear exactly whom the *Jewish Chronicle* had in mind when referring to 'the community', but it did not appear to encompass the working class Jew.

The Committee decided to form branches in all parts of London to assist in money-raising. They also looked to the small synagogues for support, but this never did materialise. The first well known figure to be recruited was Sigmund Fineman, the Yiddish actor and playwright, who promised an annual subscription of £52 and free use of the Pavilion Theatre on Sundays for the purpose of propaganda, collecting subscriptions, and recruiting workers. In June it was announced to an enthusiastic and crowded meeting held at St. George's Hall, Cable Street, Berliner presiding, that they already had more than 3,000 members. Three branches had been established and others were projected.

Another well-attended meeting was held a month later at Princes Hall, Commercial Road and the name, the East London Jewish Hospital Association, was used for the first time. The *Jewish Chronicle* reported[4] that comment had been made on the fact that even though none of the community's influential workers had come forward to offer assistance, this had by no means diminished the enthusiasm of the organisers. Even a junior committee of boys under fourteen years of age had been formed, and some of its members addressed the meeting. One said that notwithstanding their youth, they could understand the usefulness of, and need for, a Jewish hospital which would avoid the necessity for them having to lose time from school, which they now did when accompanying non-English speaking relatives to the hospitals. Mrs Levy, speaking at a meeting of the Ladies' Branch at Cannon Street Road Synagogue, was defiant. She said that although there was much opposition, the Committee had no doubt as to the ultimate success of the scheme. As she said on a later occasion,[5] 'the greater the struggle, the greater the victory'. The balance sheet showed they had received £35 from penny subscriptions alone.

A Central Committee, consisting of delegates representing the various branches, met in October 1907. They were told that there was £300 in hand, and the scheme, which by now had the open support of several local general practitioners, was progressing satisfactorily. The officers elected were: President: Isador Berliner; Vice-President Mrs Levy: Treasurer, Jacob Suyeta: Trustees, Mrs Sirota and Mrs Frazer: and Hon. Secretary, Nathan Jacobowicz. One of this number was to turn against them later.

Each month brought news of the establishment of fresh branches, at Stoke Newington, Finsbury Park and elsewhere, including, most significantly, a branch in the West End. This meant that support was now coming from some of the more affluent members of the community; the East End poor were no longer struggling entirely alone. In recognition of this, the Committee changed the name of the organisation from the East London Jewish Hospital Association to the London Jewish Hospital Association. It operated from 16 Nelson Street, the address of the secretary.

The early part of 1908 was a period of quiet progress, and an attempt was made to secure the support of Israel Zangwill, the novelist, playwright and leading Zionist. In a letter to him of 2 April 1908, one of the Committee members wrote:

> Many needs have accumulated during the last twenty years amongst the Yiddish-speaking population of London, numbering over 100,000.
>
> The most glaring need is at present a small Jewish hospital for patients who do not speak English. In order to get a part of the necessary funds, a Grand Concert will be held at the Queen's Hall, on Saturday evening, May 23rd.
>
> Very prominent Artists, such as the Great Violinist Zimbalist, Prof. Auer (of St Petersburg), Miss Irene Sharrer, Miss Cassel, and the London Symphony Orchestra have been kind enough to offer their services free.
>
> To crown the success of this Concert, we need your patronage and influence. A reply at an early date will be esteemed.
>
> Faithfully yours,
> I. Perkoff.

Interestingly, these working class men had organised a classical concert for their first major fund raising effort, and had persuaded international artists to appear. Zangwill replied on 5 April from the offices of the Jewish Territorial Organisation:

I congratulate you on the splendid concert you are arranging, but I am afraid I cannot appear in the role of patron. The reason is that I take this title seriously, and I have not yet become convinced that the plan you are so splendidly attempting is feasible. You may not be aware that my co-operation in this movement was sought at the beginning. I refused mainly because I have even more important work to do for the Jewish people which takes all my time, but I also considered that the cost of an efficient hospital was so colossal that it was beyond the power of the East End to endow one adequately. There is a Jewish hospital in Manchester, but it is small and I do not believe they can afford all the efficient medical contrivances that are necessary in a model hospital. If the Jewish wards of the existing hospitals are really unsatisfactory, then pressure could have been brought to bear to improve them by threatening to withdraw Jewish subscriptions. I do not wish to discourage you, and I greatly admire the energy of your efforts, but all the same I must leave the Ghetto to work out its own problem.

I cannot in the least see why patrons are necessary, and why the East End cannot attend a concert for this purpose without an array of names.

With best wishes,
Israel Zangwill.

At a Central Committee meeting in November, Berliner announced that they were negotiating for a site in Stepney Green, consisting of 22,000 square feet of ground and five houses. It was large enough to allow for additions to be made from time to time, wing by wing, so as ultimately to make it equal to any hospital then existing. It was close to the heart of the Yiddish-speaking section of the community, and easily accessible from all parts of the East End. Stepney Green underground station was nearby, and numbers 9a, 10, 10a, 25 and 25a buses, and numbers 61 and 66 trams stopped within two minutes' walk.

The owner was Frederick Charrington, the heir of the prosperous brewery family and evangelical crusader against drink and vice. He was sympathetic to their cause, and offered to sell for £6,500. The Committee had £950 in hand, and Berliner said, optimistically, that as soon as this reached £1,000 to cover the deposit, the balance could quickly be raised by bazaars and concerts. Jane Gourvitch, a neighbour of Berliner, who was twelve years old, and a member of the Children's Branch, wrote to the *Jewish Chronicle*[6] asking for support to enable her to reach her target of collecting 100,000 farthings.

To help the funds, cinematograph displays had been arranged for every Sunday at the Pavilion Theatre, and other functions were also announced. A month later

Berliner, at a meeting with Mr. Wedgwood Benn M.P. on the platform, was able to announce that they were on the point of exchanging contracts at a reduced price of £5,400 – the result of heavy bargaining with Charrington. In only eighteen months, he said – (it was nearer twenty-four) – they had raised £1,100, and weekly subscriptions now totalled £40:

> We do not wait for the support of our rich co-religionists – that will come in good time; it will be by our own efforts and our own enthusiasm that we must achieve success. We are full of gratitude to the London Hospital and other hospitals for what is done for our brethren, but we want a Jewish hospital with Jewish doctors and Jewish nurses, and even a Jewish porter, in order that our brothers and sisters who are afflicted can make themselves easily understood and can gain the confidence engendered from the converse in a tongue with which they are familiar. We all realised the hostility with which such a movement would be regarded by the richer Jews, but I am quite confident that once we are established help of all kinds will come from all quarters.[7]

Berliner prophesied that those who then opposed would become their warmest friends and supporters. 'Converts are always most keen', he said, 'once they are converted'.

His speech showed remarkable ebullience, confidence, and considering the difficulties they faced, an almost childlike innocence. After nearly two years, they had collected less than one fifth of the cost of the land, had nothing towards the cost of the building, and the grand total of £40 per week subscriptions towards the maintenance of a hospital in London and all that that entailed. But he and his friends had a stubborn determination and a willingness to face the odds.

Those opposing the scheme had not yet fully opened fire - there had hardly been any need as the advance towards the projected goal was so slow. But behind the scenes Lord Rothschild had already made it quite clear to his friends that he did not intend to support the scheme and did not want them to do so. Now that there was a semblance of progress, the opponents were to come out into the open and fire their first heavy salvoes.

The *Jewish Chronicle* of 25 December 1908 gave space to an interview with E. W. Morris, the Secretary of the London Hospital and Viscount Knutsford's right-hand man. He damned the scheme with quiet condescension. He had, he said, followed it with anxious interest, but, although appreciating the sentimental considerations that had actuated his 'Jewish East End friends', and although admiring their motives, he had the utmost misgivings:

> These good folk are underestimating the obstacles and difficulties with which they will have to contend. Finance will be their big problem, since even well established voluntary

hospitals are living from hand to mouth. They will not be able to afford the equipment, and there will not be enough sufficiently qualified Jewish doctors available to them, as there are not many Jewish consultants and they are in any event engaged at existing hospitals. The same applies to Jewish nurses. The London Hospital attends to every reasonable religious and other want of its very large number of Jewish in-patients and out-patients. It is most unlikely that the large hospital funds, the King Edward's, the Saturday, and Sunday Hospital Funds will assist, because they discouraged new institutions. Money used for the purpose of the scheme will probably be squandered. Also anything that has the tendency of crippling the finances of existing hospitals will bring the day nearer when the hospitals will have to pass under state control, and that will be a great national disaster and a gross waste of public money.

He suggested there should be a conference between his House Committee and the representatives of the London Jewish Hospital Association, as he felt the promoters were unaware of all the work done for Jews by the London Hospital. He made the point that Manchester did not provide a true analogy, because there none of the general hospitals had made special provision for Jewish patients.

This interview was followed by an article in the diary column of the *Jewish Chronicle* by 'Tatler', the nom-de-plume of Rev A. A. Green of the Hampstead Synagogue.[8] Thirty years earlier, his father, Rev Aaron Levy Green [1821–83] had been one of the most prominent supporters of The Society for supporting the Destitute Sick, and was a signatory to a manifesto calling for a Jewish hospital in London,[9] but the son did not follow in his father's footsteps. 'Tatler' disapproved of the scheme, and urged the promoters to consider Morris's words most carefully. What the supporters should do, he said – and throughout the campaign there was no shortage of advice from their opponents as to how their funds should be used – was to consider establishing a nursing home.

In May 1909, the Committee decided to put its affairs into a limited company, and the London Jewish Hospital Association Ltd was incorporated. Its twenty-five subscribers included a good cross-section of East End Jewry, the majority living within walking distance of each other:

I. Berliner, 163 Cannon Street Road, Hairdresser
M. Cohen, 72 St George's Street, Master Tailor
J. Coopernick, 31 Wellesley Street, Furrier
R. Donofsky, 39 Langdale Street, Ink Manufacturer
Anton Fischer, 167 Commercial Street, Restaurateur
J. Franck, 18 Widegate Street, Tailor
Louis M. Greenberg, 17 Deal Street, Tailor
L. Haffkin, 72 Oxford Street, Mohel
M. Haimovich, 57 Cable Street, Stick Maker
L. Herscowitz, 16 Nelson Street, Compositor

N. Jacobowicz, 16 Nelson Street, Compositor
L. Lewis, 5 Nottingham Place, Waterproof Maker
J. L. Meek, 39 Archer Street, Bayswater, Master Baker
Philip Mendel, 147 Ledbury Street, Tailor
I. Perkoff, 186 Commercial Street, Photographer
A. Rayman, 40 Archer Street, Bayswater, Married Woman
H. Rosen, 4 Great Prescott Street, Book-keeper
Lewis Spector, 64 St George's Street, Master Tailor
H. Sterling, 43 Buross Street, Presser
Philip Stokolsky, 22 Gloucester Buildings, Tailor
John Straker, 45A Fashion Street, Rubber Stamp Maker
P. Van Gelder, 80 Cannon Street Road, Butcher
P. D. Weisbloom, 41 Richmond Road, Tottenham, Clerk
Lewis Wexler, 21 Winterton Street, Student
A. Zackim, 77 Varden Street, Jeweller

Only three of the twenty-five subscribers were naturalised, Berliner, Meek, and Jacobowicz. Jacobowicz was born in Lodz of Russian parents, and Meek in Shuckee, West Russia. It is safe to assume that most of the others had a Polish or Russian background.

The principal objects of the company, as set out in its Memorandum of Association, were to take over the property of the London Jewish Hospital Association and:

> provide free hospital accommodation for the poor of London, to receive paying patients, and to send out trained nurses for private nursing in London or elsewhere; to employ medical, surgical and pharmaceutical officers, nurses and attendants ... who shall speak the Yiddish language ...

The Articles provided that notices could be served on the subscribers by advertisements in the current issue of two or three papers of which at least one had to be printed in Yiddish.

The Barnato Legacy: Greenberg Speaks

Two highly significant events then occurred. First, it was learned that Henry Barnato, whose fortune had been made in South Africa, had left a legacy of £250,000 to his executors for the funding of a hospital, and rumours were circulating that they were considering using these monies for the purposes of a Jewish Hospital in London. Second, on 8 January 1909, in the issue immediately following Rev. Green's article, there was a complete reversal in the editorial attitude of the *Jewish Chronicle*, as unexpected as it was sudden. The paper had opposed the Manchester scheme and the efforts of the London Jewish Hospital Association, yet here was an editorial that not only came down on the side of the promoters of the scheme, but got to the root of the debate:

We are told by one correspondent that the establishment of a Jewish Hospital would show 'a painful feeling of ingratitude' by our people towards the great general hospitals which are now used by Jews and non-Jews alike. If a Jewish Hospital were founded Jews would be able to relieve these hospitals of some of the expense in which they are now involved by what they do for Jewish patients. Where, can it reasonably be contended, would be the ingratitude in this? Nor must it be forgotten that Jews have always – and it has merely been their duty – generously supported these hospitals, and there is no reason to suppose that they would not continue doing so because of the establishment of an institution which was specifically Jewish.

Nor is it a valid argument to suggest that the Barnato money could be used for some other purpose, That argument could be extended to cover any number of purposes which, however, do not happen to be within the testator's ideas. The fact of the matter is, the whole question is, how much will a Jewish hospital be financially supported? If sufficient funds be forthcoming, then there does not appear to be any reason why a Jewish hospital should not be founded here in London as there has been in Manchester, and it would undoubtedly supply a keenly felt want.

The only danger to the proposal is that it may be started on a small scale before sufficient funds are available whereby the best and most up-to-date treatment may be given, such as is accorded to patients in the great general hospitals in the metropolis. And here we make bold to throw out a suggestion. They [the Joels] could now, with the legacy of Mr Barnato as a nucleus, themselves add to it and thus provide for a fund which would allow for the institution of a Jewish hospital in the East End of London large enough not only to accommodate at least a fair proportion of the patients for whom it could cater, but large enough also to be a school of medicine and surgery, and important enough to attract Jews who practise the profession of the healing art. We have in London no dearth of medical talent, and there can be no question that to many of our co-religionists, stricken with disease or accident, a hospital entirely Jewish – with Jewish doctors, Jewish nurses, and Jewish kitchen and, above all, with Jewish patients – would be a real boon.

We throw out the hint to Messrs Joel because we believe they would be as anxious as the late Mr Barnato to perpetuate the name under which they have so greatly prospered. Needless to say, before anything could be done in the matter a very strong committee formed by leading members of the community, both lay and medical, would have to formulate a scheme which whilst adequately fulfilling the objects of a Jewish hospital, would tend to do nothing in the very slightest to wean away from the other hospitals any of the Jewish support which they now obtain. Indeed, even under the most favourable circumstances, Jews would still have to rely upon the general hospitals for relief to their poor brethren.

59

The editorial was written by Leopold Greenberg. He had waited some time before making his personal views known, but once he acted it was with dramatic effect. His editorial was incisive. Whatever sophisticated reasons were given by the supporters of the scheme, their basic wish was to have a hospital with a specifically Jewish atmosphere, and that required all the ingredients he set out. What really worried the opponents, was that the separate establishment of a Jewish hospital might alienate the non-Jewish elements in society. It could also lead to the diminution of Jewish support for the general hospitals; and that, in turn, might lead to the exclusion of the poor Jew from the general hospitals. Importantly for the Jewish establishment, it might also to some extent take the leadership and control of the community out of their hands.

Greenberg had cleverly tried to allay the fears of both sides, indicating to the community leaders that they could take over the Committee if they would genuinely work for a Jewish hospital, and telling the Committee that if they accepted the participation of the community leaders they could achieve their objective of having a Jewish hospital.

It was typical of Greenberg to 'throw out a hint' to the Joel family as to what they should do with their money. He was never backward in using the columns of the *Jewish Chronicle* to provoke the rich into supporting charitable causes he thought should be supported. In appropriate cases he headed details regarding the wills of the wealthy – 'to charity, nil' – in an attempt to shame those who would follow to avoid such posthumous bad publicity. Shortly afterwards, Rev Green's column ceased, and 'Mentor', who was Greenberg, took over.

Addressing the fear that a Jewish hospital might cause anti-Semitism, Dr B. Gortein wrote:[10]

> And why is a hospital for sick Jews objected to in some quarters? Because some Englishmen of the Jewish persuasion are afraid it might produce a certain amount of ill-feeling among the Gentiles, perhaps even a little anti-Semitism. When Herzl launched his immortal plan of an autonomous home for the poor persecuted Jews, a similar outcry was raised against his idea, and fear and anguish seized many faint-hearted Jews lest anti-Semitism might become rampant. But Zionism has improved the self-respect of some of the Jewish people and has, I venture to say, even gained us the esteem and regard of a great many Gentiles. Similarly, the building of a hospital in a grand and imposing style, equipped with the latest modern requirements, provided with an excellent staff of Yiddish-speaking doctors and skilled Jewish nurses, could only bring honour to English Jewry.

He had highlighted another division within Anglo-Jewry, between those who preferred that the community should keep its head below the parapet and adopt a low profile at all times so as not to stir up anti-Semitism, and those who believed that openness was more desirable and effective.

Shortly following this, Anghel Gaster in a powerful speech made at an Association meeting at Ladbroke Hall, commented on the current use of communal funds:[11]

> I see the United Synagogue is going to spend about £40,000 for the erection of another place of worship. Would it not be much more gratifying in God's sight to devote that money towards the erection of a Jewish hospital, which is so urgently needed? What would be of greater benefit to our community, another synagogue – where during the greater part of the year the seats are mostly vacant – or a hospital? How many useful lives would be saved by it? How many homes would be made happy by it? How much pain and suffering would be saved by it? Could you contemplate for a moment the contingency of having empty beds in it, when all the hospitals are so overcrowded for lack of accommodation? Does not the fervent Jew pray quite as fervently at home as in a synagogue? Which could he be deprived of more easily – a hospital or a synagogue? Is it right to attend to their souls and leave their bodies to rot?

Goodman Levy, who was now very actively engaged in the Committee's work, secured a meeting with Jack Barnato Joel, and followed this with a letter. Joel's reply of 26 February was not encouraging.[12] He indicated that he and his co-trustees were all 'more or less' against the establishment of a Jewish hospital; they thought it 'would be most unwise'.

In the course of a letter to the *Jewish Chronicle*[13] Dr J. Snowman, who had studied at the London Hospital and practised in the East End, wrote:

> The rumour that the trustees of the Barnato bequest are considering with some favour the proposal to build a Jewish Hospital, puts a new complexion upon the possibilities of the matter. It casts a gleam of hope upon a despondent outlook. But powerful appeals have been pressed upon the Barnato trustees from other quarters, and the public cannot presume to know which claims will prevail.

It was a timely warning, and left the reader guessing who had made the 'powerful appeals'; but Goodman Levy had not received an outright rejection, and some hope remained. It is noteworthy that Levy, a more establishment figure, had been chosen to meet Joel, and not Berliner.

The *Jewish Chronicle* continued to give balanced space to both sides of the argument in its correspondence columns and in interviews. Generally speaking, those who were closely involved with existing hospitals as donors, subscribers, vice-presidents, house committee members, members of aid societies, and visiting ministers, were against the scheme. One of them, Rev S. Levy of Great St Helen's Synagogue, who had twelve years experience as a visiting minister at the London Hospital, made some telling points.[14] The language difficulty, he claimed, was greatly exaggerated. Of the 1,510 Jewish in-patients at the London Hospital in 1907 many of them knew only English, and could not speak or understand Yiddish; many spoke both languages; and comparatively few spoke Yiddish only. Further, the Jewish population of the East End was either stationary or diminishing. He said it was remarkable with what rapidity the second generation entirely discarded Yiddish. 'Yiddish may never become extinct, but it will gradually become more or less restricted to the adults who, in the course of nature, will be replaced by their English-speaking children'; and even if the hospital found sufficient Jewish doctors, what guarantee, he asked, was there that they would speak Yiddish? To this, another correspondent retorted that far from Yiddish dying out there were a large number of weeklies, and three daily Yiddish papers compared with only one five years earlier.

Dr. J. Snowman, in his letter mentioned earlier, said he was sure the governors and members of house committees of hospitals did all they could to ensure equal treatment for Jews and non-Jews, but it was not enough that those men (they were invariably men) who were behind the scenes should be sympathetic and high minded. In a hospital it was essential that such sentiments should also sway the house surgeons and physicians, sisters and nurses, even attendants and porters. They were a 'fleeting host' whose Jewish sympathies were often ill-developed, but it was they who came into contact with the Jewish patients, not the members of the house committees. He added:

> I make bold to say that the British working man who staggers into a casualty department late on Saturday night suffering from a scalp wound sustained in a drunken brawl, is infinitely more welcome than the uncouth immigrant Jew who shuffles in, in a piteous plight, complaining of something which the medical officer on duty cannot understand. The hospital administration may enjoin equal social treatment, but it cannot command, from the whole active staff, the same sympathy with the Russo-Polish Jews as is accorded to the native Britisher.

He added that the majority of Jewish doctors and students who had worked in hospitals with Jewish patients favoured the establishment of a Jewish hospital.

Mrs Levy suggested a compromise. She said the Association would be quite content to be under the suzerainty and control of the London Hospital. The London could deal with the English-speaking patients, and the Jewish Hospital could deal with the others. They could work hand in glove, the London Hospital taking the more difficult cases. Yiddish-speaking doctors and nurses would be available in an emergency for the London to call in. She added:

> It is true that the leaders of the community are at present against us, but I do not despair on that account. We have the backing of the working classes. Those magnificent institutions, the Home for Aged Jews and the Home for Jewish Incurables, were started by working men, and I derive considerable encouragement from that fact.

The reference to the Home for Aged Jews, originally a Jewish workhouse, was particularly apposite, as it had many parallels with the Jewish hospital movement.[15] It was led by Solomon Green, known as 'Sholey' Green, an East End tradesman who was determined to establish a Jewish workhouse to avoid the necessity for impoverished Jews having to enter a parochial workhouse. With the assistance of 'a few worthy men of the working class' living in the East End, he determined to face and overcome any obstacles placed in his way by the leaders of the community and the entrenched interests of existing institutions. But whereas Berliner was a quiet, dogged, thoughtful individual, Green sometimes mistook invective for oratory, and his forceful language drove away some who might otherwise have helped him. He originally formulated the idea in 1864, but his first efforts failed. He was told that his scheme was unnecessary, and that it would lead to an invasion by foreign Jews clamouring for a place. He tried to arrange a meeting with the Jewish Board of Guardians, but they would not see him. None of the wealthy Jews would back him. He was discouraged, even reviled, by his cousin, the Rev A. L. Green, who was then writing in the *Jewish Chronicle* under the nom-de-plume 'Nemo'. He described Sholey and his supporters as 'grossly ignorant and defiantly irreligious. The advocacy of this class of men only distances thinkers, givers and doers'.[16] In 1871 Sholey Green made a further determined effort. He established that there were only twenty-three Jews in London workhouses, of whom nine were in the Whitechapel Workhouse. He addressed a meeting held on 5 March 1871 in the Vestry Room of Princes (later Princelet) Street Synagogue:

> Let us begin as our fathers did. The Orphan Asylum was started in Petticoat Lane, the Aged Needy in the same neighbourhood and the Widows' Home also. But when these societies were in good working order, then the rich man came and took them over from the poor man, and brought them, by reason of their wealth, to success. Let us start a workhouse – we can do it, we poor people can do it. Assist us, and I am sure we shall have, before long, a Jewish Workhouse.

Within weeks the movement had 1,900 subscribers, all from the poorer class, paying one penny to threepence per week. They took speedy and decisive action. On 4 April a temporary home was opened at 123 Wentworth Street, and fourteen people were taken in, six from Whitechapel Workhouse, four from Homerton, two from Bow, and one each from Windsor and Sheerness. On 5 May, they sent a deputation to the President of the Poor Law Board, the Right Honourable C. J. Stanfeld, seeking approval for payments from the workhouse guardians equal to their savings occasioned by the transfers. This was agreed in the case of the Whitechapel Guardians, on condition that the Institution submitted to the supervision of the Board. In their first year they raised £600, and received thirty-one persons into the Home, with an average of twenty residents at any one time. Green and his associates realised by now that they needed the assistance of the wealthy, and cultivated them. Green apologised through the press for his previous intemperate language, and the vice-President, S. E. Moss said they would be quite willing for the leaders of the community to relieve the working men of the management. Green induced the philanthropist F. D. Mocatta to associate himself with the Jewish Home, as it came to be known. Mocatta donated freehold premises in Stepney, and became President. Sholey Green remained a member of the Committee until his death in 1899.

The Orphan Asylum came into being following the great cholera epidemic of 1830. According to Cecil Roth in his *History of the Great Synagogue*, a poor couple named Assenheim died within a short time of one another, leaving three children. A cucumber seller in Petticoat Lane, Abraham Green, whose sense of pity was aroused, left his stall and went round the nearby streets, private houses and shops to find help. Carrying two of the children in his arms, and leading the third by the hand, he appealed to the local Jews until he had collected enough in his cucumber basket for a nucleus of a maintenance fund. This was the origin of the Jews' Orphan Asylum. The institution, which gained the support of Isaac Vallentine, the founder of the *Jewish Chronicle*, originally opened in St Mark's Street in Spitalfields. It later merged with the Norwood Jewish Orphanage.

These examples were an encouragement to Berliner and his friends.

On 25 January 1909, a special meeting comprising members from all branches of the Association was held at Goulston Street Baths to discuss progress and plans. 2,500 crowded in, and hundreds more lined the street unable to obtain admission. Berliner, speaking in Yiddish, announced that they had agreed to pay Charrington a deposit and complete the purchase within one year. If they had not completed by then, Charrington had agreed to allow them very generous deferred term payments.

Viscount Knutsford Speaks

Berliner further announced that through the good offices of the *Jewish Chronicle*, the conference suggested by E. W. Morris had been held with the authorities of the London Hospital on 20 January.[17] They had pledged themselves not to communicate anything that transpired, but what he could tell them was that as far as they were concerned the outcome was unsatisfactory. He did not elaborate.

At a later meeting, Berliner said that as a result of great pressure from members the Committee had reluctantly concluded that they should reveal what had happened at the conference. Berliner, Mrs Levy, Mr Jacobowicz and four others had attended on behalf of the London Jewish Hospital Association. They met members of the London Hospital House Committee, among them Knutsford, who presided, and the Hon Harry Lawson, the Jewish Mayor of Stepney.

Knutsford had said he was absolutely sure a Jewish hospital was not needed. Even if needed then, it would not be needed in a couple of years' time when the Aliens Act would be strengthened, thereby stemming the great influx of Jewish aliens into the United Kingdom. He thought an alien should learn the language of his adopted country, and if he did not – well that was his own lookout; and even if they had a Jewish Hospital they would not be able to obtain a sufficient number of Yiddish speaking doctors and nurses. To this, Mrs Levy responded that this did not present the slightest difficulty, since she was already promised the service of two or three eminent physicians and a number of nurses.

Berliner asked if, at the Association's expense, they could be accommodated in a corner of the London Hospital's building, where patients who spoke only Yiddish could receive attention at the hands of a Yiddish-speaking doctor. Knutsford replied that they had no available space. He said the most he could do was to engage the services of an interpreter, if the Association paid the cost. 'All in all', said Viscount Knutsford, 'it is a ridiculous scheme to spend a sum of upwards of a quarter of a million pounds to provide a hospital for the few Jews who do not speak English or who do not care to'.

These disclosures were greeted with great indignation. Mrs Liebster, looking back upon the meeting five years later,[18] regretted that they had approached the London Hospital. She felt it was a moment of weakness and compromise, and that they had forgotten their dignity.

If the London Hospital had seen its way clear at this stage to accommodate the new hospital within its own walls – probably the provision of just ten to twenty extra beds would have sufficed to satisfy the promoters – the conflict could have ended then and there. The Hospital authorities could, perhaps, have used one of the existing Jewish wards or perhaps an additional ward for the purpose, and at a later stage quietly brought it back within their own control, having drawn the sting from the proponents of the scheme. This would have had the advantage of bringing even greater financial support from the Jewish community.

But Viscount Knutsford was not a man to compromise, particularly when he was winning, for the promoters were almost as far away from succeeding in their ambition as they were when they had started two years earlier. Once this moment had passed, a fight to the finish was inevitable.

And what of Rothschild all the while? Until this point the opponents had little to fear, because the scheme was making such slow progress; but now that the *Jewish Chronicle* was supportive, and there was still an outside possibility that a donation would firmly establish it, they could no longer delay. Lord Rothschild's answer would shortly be given, but he waited his moment and his platform.

LORD ROTHSCHILD SPEAKS

Lord Rothschild took the opportunity to make his views publicly known to those who might still be in any doubt about them, when he addressed the Golden Jubilee Festival Dinner of the Jewish Board of Guardians:[1]

> The people who propose to set up this new charity are discontented with the work of perhaps the greatest and most charitable institution in the world, the London Hospital ... I am not betraying any confidence when I say that their hope that the hospital may be endowed with the money left by the late Mr Henry Barnato is a futile hope. I am sure it will not be given for this purpose.

He was 'sure', and was clearly speaking with inside knowledge; he would not otherwise have said so at a public meeting. He said he was 'not betraying any confidence', which must have meant that he had permission from the executors to make the statement. It was obvious that he had influenced them. He continued:

> I only wish to tell these kind-hearted but misguided people that the late Dr Asher,[2] who was connected with the Jewish Board of Guardians and the United Synagogue, always had the greatest antipathy to, and always objected to, any Jewish medical charity. He said, in his terse way, that blue pills and rhubarb had no religion ... I have ventured to address you on this subject in the hope that those who have influence will put their face against a mischievous innovation, and will justify our gratitude to institutions like the London Hospital and the Metropolitan Hospitals who have attended the Jewish sick with so much devotion and success.

There was an immediate counter-attack on Lord Rothschild's arguments from Greenberg:

> There is no man whose views on philanthropic effort we should be more inclined to defer to than those of Lord Rothschild. Himself a Prince among philanthropists his advice in such matters can only spring from his deep and heartfelt conviction as to the value or otherwise of any beneficent scheme upon which his opinion is given ... But the epigram of Dr. Asher quoted by the noble lord does not bring much logic to the argument. Blue pills and rhubarb it is true have no religion. But neither have coals and blankets, nor, indeed, as the gathering which Lord Rothschild was addressing was an eloquent reminder, has charity itself. Yet we have specifically Jewish organisations for these. It really requires a Talmudist to explain why it is right to nurse people back to health and strength in a specifically Jewish convalescent home,[3] and wrong to do so in a specifically Jewish hospital.

Greenberg said Rothschild's most forcible argument was his announcement that the Barnato legacy would not be made available for the purposes of a Jewish hospital, and that he would not support it. The question of money was vital to the hospital cause, and without adequate support to ensure the best medical and surgical treatment, nothing worthy or useful could be done. Lord Rothschild's opposition was a serious blow, but Greenberg said he thought that Lord Rothschild was not fully informed, and that the sooner the promoters set about placing all the facts before him the better it would be for them.

Viscount Knutsford had already set his face against any real form of co-operation with the promoters. Rothschild had now set out his views, widely reported, to an audience that included the community's wealthiest and most influential people. Any hope of money from the Barnato legacy was gone; instead the executors gave the £250,000 to the Middlesex Hospital for cancer research.[4] The financial difficulties were so formidable that many supporters must have felt in their bones that the prospects of their ever seeing a Jewish hospital were severely limited, and many must have been tempted to fold their tents and quietly slip away; it was a devastating moment.

The financial task that lay ahead of them was well set out in a letter from D. Phillips of Mile End Road.[5] A statistical report from the King's Fund established that the average cost per bed for a hospital in London was £80 per year, and the average cost per visit of an out-patient was 7d. Phillips calculated that if a Jewish hospital were to take over the Jewish patients treated in the London and Metropolitan hospitals it would require an annual income of £16,250. 'The Jewish Hospital Association', he wrote 'has been in existence for two and a half years, and its total funds are about £2,000, just an eighth of the sum necessary to keep a hospital for one year. Then where is the £50,000 necessary for building and equipping a hospital of this size? On the face of these facts, hard facts, not visions, I submit it is folly to continue the project'. The logic of his argument appeared to be inescapable and irrefutable.

Ernest Walford who was an original member of the Committee of the defunct Leman Street Dispensary made a further point:[6]

> The promoters of the Jewish hospital will not see that a) the 'charity fund' of the community is not inexhaustible, and that it is already strained to breaking point and b) the 'fixed charges' will be very considerable annually, and would be required to be paid before any money could be spent in curing or alleviating illness.

Reverend S. Levy confirmed this, and said[7] that the Jewish Hospital movement had not tapped new sources of revenue. It had simply succeeded in making some people change the object of their support. At domestic celebrations where collections used to be made for the Talmud Torahs, collections were instead being made for the Hospital. Consequently, many communal institutions were feeling the difference in their incomes.

But the Jewish Hospital pioneers were not daunted. On 20 August 1909, at the Pavilion theatre where, despite the very warm weather, every seat was taken, Berliner revealed that when the cheque for the deposit was ready to be signed, the Treasurer, Jacob Suyeta, refused to put his signature to it, giving as his reason what he termed 'the sound utterances' of Lord Rothschild at the Jewish Board of Guardians dinner. Anghel Gaster replaced him as treasurer and, in a fighting speech, said:

> Are we called '*am kerschey oref*', a stiff-necked people, for nothing? Will we submit blindly and be dictated to by some of the rich as to what is good for us? We will show them by our deeds and works of self-sacrifice that we are independent of the rich, and that we are determined to have a hospital of our own. We have the numbers, and we alone know the necessity for it.
>
> Is it not proof of our earnestness in this matter that we have already collected nearly £1,700 – and that in pennies only. Are we going to give it up and sit still because our Lord – I refer to our financial Lord – has pronounced it unnecessary, and whose words I understand have deterred the trustees of a late millionaire from giving us what would have been an everlasting monument to his memory – a Jewish hospital for the poor of his brethren, from whose ranks he himself had sprung? I ask you not to be disheartened; we will show the rich by our noble example what we can do.

The following week Gaster was criticised for his 'intemperate' remarks by Frederick S. Franklin, the Secretary of the Visiting Committee of the Jewish Board of Guardians and a member of the Council of the Metropolitan Hospital. Franklin said that Lord Rothschild was opposed to the scheme because it was neither necessary nor politic. It was not because the 'financial Lord' made that pronouncement that the rich were opposed to the scheme – it was because their views were identical to his.

There followed a period of long, hard, financial grind. A project was launched to issue 22,000 shares at half a guinea each 'so that the humblest supporter will have the satisfaction of knowing that by taking a share he has paid for at least a foot of ground'. Arrangements were made for the payment of these shares by subscription over a period of a year. Subscribers received a certificate signed by the President, Secretary and Treasurer, that had the company seal affixed below a coloured drawing of the hospital as they hoped it would be. Five beds were shown in two adjoining wards, or perhaps it is one ward divided into two, with a mezzuzah on the archway between them. One patient, wearing a skull cap, is seen in bed reading, and there is a visiting minister sitting by another bed. A neatly dressed nurse is giving a patient a pill, and the light and airy wards are dotted with potted plants. The heading of the certificate was 'London Jewish Hospital Association' repeated in Hebrew lettering immediately below. The subscribers, a typical cross-section of East End Jewish working men, had their names entered in a golden book. Bricks, too, were sold at sixpence each.

Eventually it was announced in December 1909 that contracts had been exchanged for the purchase of the land.[8] An initial payment of £1,500 was made, and the balance was payable over three years on mortgage from the vendor. At a meeting in Ladbroke Hall, Ladbroke Grove, Dr Gaster said that what had looked like a fairy tale or some castle in the air scheme, was now near realisation. There were over fifty Jewish doctors in London ready to devote their lives to the poor, enough to stock three or four hospitals.

So the year that had produced so many setbacks, ended on a note of high hope and buoyant confidence, but if they had known then how long and stony the road ahead was, would they have continued?

The King Edward VII Memorial Scheme

A national event occurred that was to draw attention to the movement from both inside and outside the Jewish community. In May 1910, King Edward VII died. Immediately a 'Sixpenny Fund' was launched at a meeting held at the Jewish Working Men's Club, attended by the Chief Rabbi, Dr Hermann Adler. The plan was to raise sufficient money to erect a memorial to the late King on behalf of the East End Jewish working classes, after appropriate consultation with King George V as to his wishes. Dr Adler told the meeting that he was authorised to say that Lord Rothschild supported the scheme.

At the same time, but at a meeting of the supporters of the LJHA, the bright idea was put forward of following the example of the Manchester Victoria Memorial Jewish Hospital, and calling the new hospital 'The King Edward Jewish Memorial Hospital'. Doubtless the suggestion sprang from deep loyal feelings, but the possibility it afforded for a public relations coup and for increased publicity and subscriptions, might have crossed the he mind of one or two of those present. The *Jewish Chronicle* greeted the idea warmly.[9] Rothschild and Viscount Knutsford recognised at once the possible advantage to the LJHA, and as will be seen took what they believed to be appropriate steps to crush the initiative.

The following month the proposal was put to a crowded public meeting held at the Pavilion Theatre, and for the first time the Haham graced the platform. He moved the resolution that a humble petition should be presented to King George V seeking his approval. Another formidable supporter had been won. His speech, that was to be typical of many to follow over the years, was hard hitting, abrasive, extremely provocative, and showed scant respect for other community leaders. The resolution was passed unanimously. The London Hospital's secretary, E. W. Morris, said the proposal was in the most questionable taste, an attempt to prop up an unpopular scheme by attaching to it the name of the late King.

At the beginning of August, the LJHA opened an office at 41, Stepney Green, a large house with a splendid garden that had been occupied by Frederick Charrington for many years. He had kindly agreed to give them possession before completion of the sale. The existence of a recognised centre helped to awaken those whose interest in the movement had been merely passive. In large lettering over the premises appeared the words – 'The King Edward Jewish Memorial Hospital' – a move guaranteed to infuriate their opponents.

Another crowded meeting of several hundred was held in September in the large hall on the Stepney Green site, with an overflow in the garden. The Haham lambasted the 'self-styled' leaders of the community.

> These men are well-meaning as far as they understand, but they do not understand the soul of the Jews in the East End. They have grown rich by God's blessing which they now abuse. Money is round, and it easily rolls from one to another. Who knows where the money will be in a generation? So we are not frightened by these people who will not give themselves, and try to prevent others from giving. They are either ignorant or hard-hearted, and their attitude is a tyrannical interference with the sympathies of the poor Jew of the East End.

Comment was made on this meeting in *The Hospital and Nursing Mirror* on 1 October 1910. The journal saw no advantages to Jews or the community at large from building such a special hospital:

> In view of the comparatively slight support that the whole scheme has hitherto received, we sincerely trust that the committee will not proceed with the scheme or, if it is absolutely necessary, that the purchased site must be retained for sentimental reasons, to establish an up-to-date Jewish dispensary ... the execution of the scheme would serve no useful purpose, at least at the moment, but rather, on the contrary, would increase the difficulty of those East End institutions which have done their best to grant all possible facilities to Jew [sic] patients.

It is possible, indeed probable, that Knutsford and Rothschild had directly or indirectly arranged for this to be published. A similar article appeared in the journal on 15 October 1910.

In due course the LJHA dropped the plan to name the Hospital in honour of the late King. The memorial erected by the 'Sixpenny Fund', at a cost of £850, was a stone drinking fountain with brass figures. It still stands, bearing a suitable inscription, in Whitechapel Road immediately opposite the London Hospital.

Lord Rothschild was approaching his seventieth birthday. The *Jewish Chronicle* urged him to make it notable by withdrawing his ban on the Hospital. This appeal, bearing Greenberg's hallmark, fell upon deaf ears. And so ended another year in the long struggle.

Purchase of the Stepney Green Site Completed

There was little progress in 1911. At the Annual General Meeting in May, the first accounts since they were incorporated as a limited company were presented. Berliner announced that they had now paid £3,400 towards the cost of the site, but they still needed a large-hearted philanthropist if speedy progress was to be made.

In another speech, delivered to the North Western Branch on 18 March 1912, the Haham said:

> I will now deal with what, from many points of view, is the real, if not the only, reason for the establishment of the hospital – the whole Jewish atmosphere ... There is a language of the mouth; but there is also a language of the heart which cannot be translated into words. The language of the heart is that of people in common with one another, and is more eloquent than any words spoken from the mouth. This creates kinship, and it is one of the reasons why a Jew feels himself as alienated in a Christian hospital. Their way of feeling is different from our way of feeling. Their way of thinking is different to our way of thinking. No less sincere; no less true; but not akin. A patient easy at heart is already half-way to a cure.

The word 'atmosphere' was to be repeated many times in connection with the Hospital.

By May 1912 the freehold had been acquired. A Building Committee was established that included Goodman Levy, Dr Mandel and Dr Anghel Gaster, and an estimate of £14,000 for the building had been received. The plans provided for a large out-patient hall to accommodate 200 and, to begin with, forty beds for in-patients. It was intended to staff the hospital with Jewish doctors, nurses and administrators. Dr Mandel said the site would eventually accommodate 180 beds.

Attempts were made to secure support from the King's Fund, a somewhat forlorn hope given the influence that Rothschild and Knutsford wielded in the organisation. Dr Mandel informed the Fund of their plans, and explained that the Hospital would be non-sectarian, but devised to meet the special requirements of the Jewish community.[10] The Fund's Secretary replied that its rules did not permit them to assist in the foundation of new hospitals, nor did it entertain applications for grants from hospitals that had not been in existence for a period of at least three years; but so that there could be no doubt about its attitude to the proposed hospital, the Secretary gratuitously added that 'in the opinion of the Committee even if any special hospital is required for Jews in East London the proposed site would seem to be in too close proximity to the London Hospital'.

Mandel replied that as most of the money for the Hospital had been contributed by thousands of the poorest inhabitants of the East End, many of whom possessed tiny fractions of the ground for which they entertained strong, sentimental interests, any proposal to move the site would provoke serious dissatisfaction. Nathan Jacobowicz also wrote, and asked whether failure to move elsewhere would preclude future support from the Fund. The Fund's response was that its Committee did not consider any good purpose would be served by the submission of further applications.

In July 1913, J. Courtney Buchanan, the Secretary and a Governor of the Metropolitan Hospital, unwisely entered into the argument. He said that Jews should consider supporting existing hospitals which already made full provision for Jewish needs, rather than give their money to the LJHA. This afforded Goodman Levy the opportunity to emphasise the point that what really concerned existing hospitals was their fear that they could be adversely affected financially should a Jewish hospital be opened:[11]

> In some respects this comment of the committee of the Metropolitan Hospital is a welcome one, for it lays open to the public view the bare bones of this controversy. It is perhaps well that the community should have the opportunity for recognising the bitter financial competition which sometimes underlies charitable questions and which is, without a doubt, the true source of the stream of obloquy which has been so lavishly poured out upon the Jewish Hospital movement. I have always held that the Jewish Hospital movement has from its very inception been sacrificed to the supposed financial interests of the Metropolitan Hospital and the London Hospital, and I will leave it to your readers to judge how far this opinion is justified.

Goodman Levy was given the task of approaching leading figures of the Jewish establishment for help, but soon found they were still implacably opposed to the scheme. Claude Montefiore refused to meet him, saying it would be a waste of time for both of them, since he was 'absolutely unable to give anything to, or to support, the proposed Jewish Hospital in London'. Lord Swaythling said he would have been delighted to meet Goodman Levy 'but for the fact that I am strongly opposed to the proposed Hospital for Jews in the East End, and would use any influence I have to prevent its being established'. Meyer Spielman wrote that he too was strongly opposed, for many reasons:

> If it were erected, which seems problematical, the whole of the Jews who can afford to give are opposed, so it would do a serious injury to our poorer co-religionist. The best medical treatment and the best nursing would be denied them, and the large number that frequent the other hospitals would be unwelcome there. Such a Jewish Hospital in the view of the attitude of the people who can give, could only be very small and therefore admit a very small number, and the majority of sufferers would be affected. There is moreover no need for such a hospital considering that the other hospitals give all the necessary facilities and there are I understand very few trained Jewish nurses. You will therefore see that I am unable to comply with your request. I may add that my brother is also opposed, which is the attitude I think of all my friends.[12]

Events began to move a little more rapidly in 1913, but despite all their public optimism the Association must still have had doubts as to its ability to finance its operation, because in April an approach was made to the London Hospital asking whether its House Committee would be willing to agree that the Jewish Hospital should become a Jewish Branch of the London Hospital. The London Hospital House Committee would not agree to the suggestion.[13]

It was not helpful that at this moment the Manchester Victoria Jewish Memorial Hospital had run into severe financial difficulties and had made an urgent appeal for help in the *Jewish World*:[14]

> The Manchester Hospital represents the most serious effort yet in this country to maintain a separate place for the treatment of the Jewish sick. If in the long run it should fail, owing to lack of funds, or what is more serious still, if inadequate funding should make its handling of the sick a byword of reproach, not only would any possibility of repeating the experiment in London or elsewhere be at an end, but a blow might be inflicted on the Jews' good name and prestige.

In June it was announced that it had been decided to start with a hospital initially requiring £10,000, and not £22,000 as previously intended. This seems the have been a wise decision, for further delay would probably have led to the movement losing its momentum. They had done well to keep the faith of their supporters for so long, with little concrete to show for it. As Mr Wedgewood Benn had perceptively pointed out, one of the most remarkable aspects of the campaign was that its supporters had gone on subscribing for so many years in good faith, not seeing what they were paying for, but trusting Berliner and his associates implicitly, and believing they would eventually see a Jewish hospital erected in the East End.[15]

At the beginning of January 1914, the old house on the site was demolished. The 7th Annual General Meeting was held in early May, and Berliner said that but for a builders' strike work on the new building would already have commenced. The *Jewish Chronicle* made a last minute attempt to bridge the gap between the opposing parties, directly appealing to the wealthy:[16]

> The Jewish Hospital movement is making substantial progress. In spite of the hostility shown in various quarters, the promoters have never looked back. Penny by penny, and shilling by shilling, the funds have accumulated ... it must be obvious to the most determined of opponents that the project has been launched in a serious and practical spirit and will be persevered with to the end. That being so, these gentlemen may well be asked whether the time has not come when they may well reconsider their attitude towards the movement. Argument was all very well at a time when the scheme existed only on paper, or in the minds and desires of enthusiasts. But now that land has been acquired and building is about to begin, would it not be more chivalrous and wise to offer help, so that the institution which is soon to arise in our midst, may accomplish its mission well, and not indifferently, and be a source of credit to the community.

At this very time, work costing £500,000 was beginning at Mount Sinai Hospital in New York; the Frankfort community subscribed £40,000 for a Jewish Hospital; and a Jewish Hospital opened in Berlin with 250 beds on a site costing £240,000. The *Jewish World* asked rhetorically, 'If a Jewish hospital is right in principle in New York, how can it be wrong in London?', and commented that it was curious that there could be such a thing as 'Jewish pain' only on the Continent and in America.

At the AGM, Mrs Leibster launched an attack on the Jewish clergy, complaining that if only the Association had the ministers on its side the fortunes of the movement would be made. She alleged the clergy did not have the courage to risk their bread and butter by speaking for the Hospital. Rev S. Levy responded, tit-for-tat, that when the wife of a Jewish doctor urged the cause of the Jewish Hospital she might be thinking of her own, or her husband's, bread and butter. In a letter to the *Jewish Chronicle*,[17] he wrote that ministers would be the first to rejoice if Mrs Leibster's tribute to their influence were founded on fact. He said the clergy, as the laymen, were divided on this issue, and he did not know of the slightest risk that any minister would run if he chose to advocate the claims of the Jewish hospital.

To this Mrs Leibster raised the question why, if there were some ministers who were for a Jewish Hospital, their voices had remained silent? If they ran no risk, why did they not speak out? And Mr Gugenheimer, in his letter quoted earlier, said that during the seven years the movement had been going on, not a single minister of the United Synagogue spoke in favour of the scheme. When the London Jewish

Hospital Association had called a conference of ministers and lay representatives of all the synagogue and benefit societies, not a single United Synagogue minister attended. The Chief Rabbi, Dr Hermann Adler had not spoken publicly, nor, as far as can be ascertained, privately, in favour of the movement, and indeed he probably opposed the idea. In 1900, when he accepted the Deed of Trust to the kosher kitchen at the German Hospital, he had remarked that it 'saves the Jewish community from the necessity of establishing a separate hospital'.[18]

Rev W. Esterson of the Hambro Synagogue pointed out that he had written to the *Jewish Chronicle* on 5 Feb 1909 in favour of the scheme before Mrs Leibster became prominent in the movement, and had taken every opportunity to advocate its cause. However no other minister joined the debate, which rather proved Mrs Leibster's point.

In the last week of July, Berliner reported that agreement had been reached with the striking workers; a contract signed with the builders, Messrs Patman and Fotheringham; and work would begin on Wednesday 5 August 1914. At long last the perseverance, patience and hard work of the founders, of the workers on the LJHA central committee and branch committees, and of the thousands of members and supporters who had raised the necessary monies by whist drives, boxing tournaments, dances, dinners, river trips, fetes, cinema performances and all the many other fund-raising activities over a period of nearly seven years were, against all the odds, to reap their reward.

Far greater events intervened; the First World War started. Subscriptions immediately fell from £60 to £20 per week. The Building Sub-Committee recommended that building operations should be suspended for a short period. It was agreed that all energies would be channelled into the war effort.

DEATH OF LORD ROTHSCHILD –
WHY HE OPPOSED

As the war progressed, hospitals became overcrowded with military wounded. There was an influx of French and Belgian Jews into the East End and the West End, and because of the lack of civilian hospital beds many of them attended the missionary dispensaries. This created uneasiness amongst the Association's members, and they brought pressure to bear on the Committee to do something about it. Some threatened to withhold future contributions unless building was resumed. In April, after due consideration, the Building Sub-Committee ordered work to restart. They decided to begin with the out-patient department only.

Just a few weeks earlier, on Wednesday 21 March 1915, Lord Rothschild, their chief adversary, died. The *Jewish Chronicle* described him as the community's 'father, guide, and friend. The man to whom all Jewry looked for help and leading'. After allowing for the lapse of a decent interval from the funeral, Greenberg addressed himself to the question of why Lord Rothschild had been so strongly opposed to a Jewish Hospital. He said[1] it had been suggested that Lord Rothschild opposed the movement because he was not in sympathy with, and had no confidence in, Berliner and his colleagues. Greenberg dismissed this without hesitation, because Rothschild knew how to save a good object from a bad worker, and would have remedied that fault, if indeed there were such a fault. To suggest that he opposed it because it was an East End movement and not a West End movement was ridiculous. He said that Lord Rothschild was 'an East End man' in Jewish politics, and regarded the needs of the East End Jews as of great importance.

So why then, Greenberg asked, was Rothschild so steadfastly opposed, an opposition that had been bitter, relentless, and unswerving? He said it was of great importance to discover the reason, for once known it could be the means of overcoming what opposition was left in the community:

> Lord Rothschild was above all a loyal man. If he hated anything more than another it was the doing of a mean trick or an unfair action. As lay head of the Jewish community he had to a large extent pledged the community to support the general hospitals, chief among them being the London Hospital, the bargain being that the general hospitals would throw their doors open freely to our people.

Now when the Jewish Hospital movement was first started it was looked upon in the Whitechapel Road [by the London Hospital] as something of an impertinence and something of a revolt. 'How dare you ask for this and that, when you are getting the best of everything? We know your Jewish peculiarities, but we cannot bring a great Hospital down to the level of Jewish idiosyncrasies, and you must put up with what you can get'. Lord Rothschild was doubtless at the same time advised that one of the means of beating out of the Jews their peculiar idiosyncrasies – idiosyncrasies that are very strong in regard to illness, accident, or death – would be to compel them to conform to the general regulations of a great general hospital.

The appeal was, therefore, made by the authorities of the London Hospital to Lord Rothschild upon two points, about which the latter was very keen. One was the capacity of Jews for enjoying the public institutions of the country without discrimination from the rest of its citizens, and the other his loyalty to an institution which he had pledged himself and the community to support. This, it would seem, was all there really was in the opposition of Lord Rothschild to the scheme.

Greenberg said that once Viscount Knutsford had told Rothschild that the establishment of a Jewish Hospital near to the London Hospital would be contrary to the interests of the London Hospital, and to some extent an abrogation of the understanding whereby the London Hospital had done so much for Jewish patients, Lord Rothschild had become violently opposed to the movement.

Greenberg knew most of the important people connected with the controversy, and had a journalist's insight and information. His analysis of Lord Rothschild's reasons was credible. However a different reason for Lord Rothschild's opposition was given four years later by his son.[2] He said he and his father had disagreed with the building of a Jewish hospital simply because they thought it was a separatist movement, and would tend to emphasise the differences that divided Jews from their fellow countrymen. This simple explanation also has the ring of truth. It always was the purpose of the establishment to integrate the recently arrived immigrants as soon as possible, and not divide them from their fellow citizens, and every means available to this end was used. In the minds of Lord Rothschild and others who fervently desired integration, a London Jewish Hospital would be detrimental to this aim and had to be opposed.

To put the matter into context, a reading of Rothschild's family correspondence with his Paris cousins shows that when the Jewish Hospital movement started Lord Rothschild was heavily involved in trying to alleviate the overwhelming problems of Russia's Jews, the impositions put upon them, their lack of freedom, and the pogroms. He received, almost daily, emissaries, official and private, feeding him information on the latest position. It is perhaps not surprising that, dealing as he was with Jewish matters on such a grand scale, and so aware of the different position between the Jews in Russia and the Jews in England, Rothschild opposed any such potentially separatist move as the London Jewish Hospital

Greenberg attacks Viscount Knutsford

Greenberg had not yet finished his attack. He turned on Knutsford:

And though Lord Rothschild is no more, we must not forget the authorities at the London Hospital who helped him to the position he took up. They have adhered, and still adhere, to the same illiberal, narrow and ill-considered policy that has been theirs from the very first. Lord Knutsford, who has been far more responsible for the opposition, Jewish and non-Jewish, to the Jewish Hospital movement than any man, has only been able to see with the eye of a grocer the possibility of a rival establishment starting in the same street. He knows nothing, and therefore cares nothing, about the depth of Jewish spirit, the real religious sentiments that animate Jews when such an institution as a hospital begins its work.

Viscount Knutsford immediately issued a denial:

I have read with pain and indignation the article which appeared in the *Jewish Chronicle* of May 21st signed 'Mentor'. It would be impossible more shamefully to misrepresent everything I have ever written, said, or thought, about the Jewish hospital ... It is a malevolent invention, purposely made to incite, if it were true, every righteous indignation.

He could not resist adding that he still believed that very few Jews would care to be treated at a hospital where anything but the very best skill and nursing was obtainable, and he did not think the proposed Jewish hospital could provide it. It is noteworthy that he did not deal directly with Greenberg's assertion of the agreement between him and Lord Rothschild.

On Sunday, 14 November 1915, the foundation stone was laid:[3]

THE LONDON JEWISH HOSPITAL.
This stone was laid by
Mrs FLORA SOLOMON DAVID SASSOON
On Sunday, November 14th, 1915
Isidor Berliner, Esq. President. Mrs Leopold Liebster Vice-Pres.
Emil B. Kapp, Esq. Vice-Pres, Dr. Anghel Gaster, Treasurer,
Nathan Jacobowicz, Esq. Secretary
Edwin T. Hall, Esq. (F.R.I.B.A.)
E. Stanley Hall, Esq. (M.A., A.R.I.B.A.) Architects
Messrs. Patman & Fotheringham, Ltd., Builders

The vast and enthusiastic gathering at the stone laying, at which a further £208.1.0d was raised, was composed largely of those who had worked for the previous eight years to bring their vision to realisation. The Haham, as usual, made a forceful speech[4] and dealt with the allegation made by the opponents of the scheme that the financial burden of the Hospital would be too much for the community to bear:

> I can tell them that until now the burden has been a featherweight. The community has not been burdened. The funds required for the purchase of the land have not come from those who raise the question. It is the workers, those present today, with their pennies, halfpennies and shillings, that have paid for it all, and they will go on paying. The Hospital will be built – it is already being built – and will soon open its doors to thousands seeking the advice of Jewish doctors and nurses.

First medical staff appointed

The first Annual Report of the General Court of Governors for the year 1915 was issued in July 1916. It reported that the out-patient department building had been completed two months earlier. It included a large waiting hall, medical, surgical, and special consulting rooms, a minor operating theatre, and a dispensary. It was anticipated that the contract price, together with the architects' fees, general building expenses, and the cost of outfitting the departments would be fully met without an overdraft. The construction was plain and sound, and no funds had been wasted in mere ornamental or decorative work. Treatment would be entirely free to the necessitous and the hospital would be open to all creeds and nationalities.

Dr Goodman Levy said that they were going to run the Hospital on the conventional lines of other London hospitals, and the foremost requirement was that they should be thoroughly efficient from a medical point of view. To achieve this, all members of the first medical staff had to be approved as suitable by two eminent medical men, Sir Rickman Godlee, President of the Royal Society of Medicine and Dr Frederick Taylor, President of the Royal College of Surgeons. This would ensure that the professional status of their honorary staff would be unimpeachable.

Those appointed to the Honorary Medical Staff were – Consulting Surgeon, Sir Rickman J. Godlee; Consulting Physician, Dr. Frederick Taylor; Physicians, Dr Julius Burnford and Dr Anghel Gaster; Surgeon, E. C. Hughes; Ophthalmic Surgeon, A. H. Levy; Surgeon in charge of Department for diseases of the Ear, Nose and Throat, H. A. Kisch; Pathologist, Dr David Nunes Nabarro; and Physician in charge of Electro-Therapeutical Department, Dr N. S. Finzi. They all held staff appointments in other London hospitals and had their own consulting rooms in Harley Street or Wimpole Street. Being attached to the London Jewish

Hospital gave them status, whether Jewish or non-Jewish, and presented them with an opportunity to make their skills widely known among the Jewish community.

The Committee of Management, under Goodman Levy's chairmanship, included five doctors, Burnford, Finzi, Gaster, A. H. Levy and Nabarro. The other members were Berliner, E. B. Kapp, A. Kevin, Mrs. Leibster, S. Leverick, M. Lipman, S. Strauss, J. Starr, H. Wolff, and most surprisingly, Rev A. A. Green. The former opponent had changed his mind, and was co-opted on to the Committee. The chairmen of the then eleven branches were S. Leverick, J. Starr, A. J. Goldman, M. Lazarus, P. Kamlet, Mrs. A. Levin, A. G. Goodman Levy (his wife was honorary treasurer), Mrs. M. Friedlander, Mrs. J. Straker, Miss Wilder, and Miss D. Lewis.

However, because of the exigencies of the War, particularly the absence in the Armed Forces of most of the doctors – four had commissions in the Royal Army Medical Corps, and one was serving abroad – the Hospital's doors remained closed for the whole of 1917 and 1918. Permission was given for an extension of the building, but this could not proceed for lack of funds. On 27 September 1918, Mr Albert M. Cohn of 21 Grosvenor Place wrote to the *Jewish Chronicle*:

> Some short while ago the Ministry of Pensions, convinced of the great utility of the London Jewish Hospital, intimated to the Council of Management that they would willingly permit the building operations to proceed and to advise that the existing war restrictions be released in this case. To the disgrace of London Jewry, the Council was compelled to reply that the funds of the Hospital as they at present stand do not permit of the building being completed . . . Oh, the shame of it! That the wealthy body of West End Jews should neglect and argue over what should be their pride and glory – a noble monument bringing solace and peace to suffering and pain.

In the *Jewish Chronicle* of 27 January 1919 there was a short note of possible great significance. 'A private conference to consider enlarging the interest of the community in the London Jewish Hospital was held at the residence of Mr and Mrs Maurice Cohn, at 21 Grosvenor Place, S.W.1. Lord Rothschild presided.' Who had called the meeting? Who was present? Who had persuaded the second Lord Rothschild to come? How did it happen that he was chairman? What was discussed and decided? Unfortunately, no further record of the meeting or the events leading up to it have been traced.

THE CAST

[1] *The Cousinhood* (1971), p. 132.
[2] A. E. Clark-Kennedy. *The London* (1963).
[3] *Indiscretions of a Warden* (1937), p. 148.
[4] The box, with four microphones, is on display at the Royal London Hospital Museum.
[5] *In Black and White* (1926).

[6] *Jewish Chronicle*, 3 September 1909.

[7] *Jewish Chronicle*, 10 March 1939, p. 15.

[8] For a more detailed description of his career and influence see *The Jewish Chronicle and Anglo-Jewry 1841–1991* (1994) David Cesarani.

[9] *Jewish Chronicle*, 20 March 1931.

[10] Letter dated 8 October 1908 from Jacobowicz to Levy. In University of Southampton Library Archives. Ref MS 116/145.

THE EARLY DAYS

[1] *Jewish Chronicle*, 15 February 1907.

[2] In the 1960s 3.3 beds per 1,000 was considered acceptable.

[3] 1 March 1907.

[4] 5 July 1907.

[5] *Jewish Chronicle*, 29 January 1909.

[6] 5 January 1909.

[7] *Jewish Chronicle*, 18 December 1908.

[8] 1 January 1909.

[9] Alex M. Jacob. *Transactions of the Jewish Historical Society of England, volume XXV* p. 88.

[10] *Jewish Chronicle*, 24 September 1909.

[11] *Jewish World*, 24 February 1909.

[12] At Southampton Library Archives, Ref: MS. 116/145.

[13] *Jewish Chronicle*, 5 February 1909.

[14] *Jewish Chronicle*, 22 January 1909.

[15] See *Transactions of the Jewish Historical Society of England* Volume XX, page 132 n.

[16] *Jewish Chronicle*, 3 March 1871.

[17] Minutes of this meeting are in the London Hospital Archives.

[18] *Jewish Chronicle*, 5 June 1914.

LORD ROTHSCHILD SPEAKS

[1] *Jewish Chronicle*, 19 February 1909.

[2] Dr Asher Asher was one of the doctors the Jewish Board of Guardians appointed to look after the health of the East End poor when the Board took over responsibility from the Synagogues. He was later Secretary of the Great Synagogue and of the United Synagogue.

[3] The Baroness de Hirsch home at Hampstead.

[4] A plaque commemorating the gift can be seen today by the western entrance to the Hospital.

[5] Letter in *Jewish Chronicle*, 9 October 1909.

[6] Letter in *Jewish Chronicle*, 11 July 1913.

[7] *Jewish Chronicle*, 15 May 1914.

[8] The contract was dated 1 November 1909.

[9] 25 May 1910.

[10] This letter dated 1 October 1912, and the subsequent correspondence, are at London Metropolitan Archives, ref. A/KE/252.

[11] *Jewish Chronicle*, 1 August 1913.

[12] This correspondence is at the University of Southampton Library Archives and Manuscripts under reference MS 116/145.

[13] *London Hospital House Committee Minutes*, 14 March 1913.

[14] *Jewish World*, 20 December 1912.

[15] *Jewish World*, 20 December 1912.

[16] 15 May 1914.

[17] 15 May 1914.

[18] *Hackney Gazette*, 14 December 1900.

DEATH OF LORD ROTHSCHILD – WHY HE OPPOSED

[1] *Jewish Chronicle*, 21 May 1915.

[2] *Jewish Chronicle*, 31 October 1919.

[3] The cost of the stone, including the inscription, was defrayed by H. Harris & Son Ltd of Mile End Road.

[4] *Jewish World*, 17 November 1915.

(II) *Isidor Berliner. 'A humble man, carrying on a humble vocation, who managed to carve for himself an enduring monument of which any prince might be proud'.*
[Mrs Enid Rosenberg]

(III) *Dr Alfred Goodman Levy. Austere, non-religious, he was Berliner's unlikely but effective ally.*
[Hugh Goodman Levy]

(IV) *Lord (Nathaniel) Rothschild. Adviser to governments, and the unchallenged lay leader of Anglo-Jewry, he determined to thwart Berliner's plans.*

[*Rothschild Archives*]

(V) *2nd Viscount Knutsford, Chairman of the London Hospital. 'Far more responsible for the opposition, Jewish and non-Jewish, to the Jewish Hospital movement than any man'.*

[*Portrait at the London Hospital*]

The Stepney Green site was just a mile away from the London Hospital.

(VI)

(IX)   *Exterior of Manchester Victoria Memorial Jewish Hospital.*

(X) *Mr and Mrs Winston Churchill arrive for the opening of the Manchester Victoria Memorial Jewish Hospital's new out-patient department in October 1908.*   *[Jewish World, 15 October 1908]*

(XI) *The working class Jewish immigrant East Enders responded to this appeal, but few others.*
[Jewish World, 28 January 1910]

(XII)   *[Mr Brian Gordon]*

(XIII)   *[Jewish World, March 7, 1913]*

London Jewish Hospital Association.

BRANCH No. 2.

ISRAEL TKATSCH

Oberkantor of the Buda-Pesth Great Temple,

With a GRAND CHOIR will officiate at

SPECIAL SERVICES

AT THE

Great Assembly Hall,

MILE END ROAD, E.

On FRIDAY and SATURDAY
the 2nd and 3rd February, 1912.

Services commence—Friday evening .... 4.30 ;
Saturday morning... 9.

•••••••••••••

Ladies and Gentlemen,

We hope you will all come to hear the world-famed Chazan TKATSCH. It is unnecessary for us to mention the remarkable qualities of his voice, as you have, no doubt, read about him in the General Press; therefore we trust you will take advantage of this opportunity to hear one of the greatest Chazonim and at the same time support a most deserving cause—the Jewish Hospital Fund.

Price of Tickets, 1/- 2/- 3/- 5/- 7/6 and 10/8, to be obtained of
Dr. A. GASTER, 88, Greencroft Gardens, West Hampstead, N.W.
Mr. I. BERLINE, 163, Cannon Street Road, E.
Mr. M. COHEN, 5, Great Alie Street, Aldgate, E. (Telephone No. 4133 London Wall).
Mr. N. JACOBOWICZ, Central Offices, 41, Stepney Green, E.
Mr. P. SIGMUND, 49, Archer Street, Bayswater, W.
Mr. BRIGHT, 2, Edward Street, Berwick Street, W.

(XV)   *[Jewish World, 19 January 1912]*

אינדעפענדענט לאנדאנער אידישע האספיטאל

London Jewish Hospital Association.

N. JACOBOWICZ,
GEN. HON. SEC.

16, Nelson Street,
Commercial Road.

London, E.   APRIL 2nd, 1908

Dear Sir,

Many needs have accumulated during the last twenty years amongst the Yiddish speaking population of London, numbering over 100,000

The most glaring need is at present A SMALL JEWISH HOSPITAL FOR PATIENTS WHO DO NOT SPEAK ENGLISH. In order to get a part of the neccessary funds, a Grand Concert will be held at the Queen's Hall, on Saturday evening, May 23rd.

Very prominent Artists, such as the Great Violinist Zimbalist, Prof. Auer (of St. Petersburg), Miss Irene Sharrer, Miss Cassel, and The London Symphony Orchestra have been kind enough to offer their services FREE.

To crown the success of this Concert, we need your patronage and influence. A reply at an early date will be esteemed.

Faithfully yours,

J. Perkiff

(XIV)   *Letter sent to Israel Zangwill, seeking patronage.*

(XVI) *Dora Schuster was one of the youngest and most indefatigable collectors for the Hospital. She later became Lady Almoner.*
        [Jewish World, 18 February 1914]

(XVII) *'Master Waxman'. He collected £30 in pennies.*
        [Jewish World, 29 November 1912]

(XVIII)   *Offices of the Association prior to the opening of the Hospital.*

[Mr Brian Gordon]

THE JEWISH WORLD

Jewish World.]
Oct. 8, 1919.

[No. 2,450.

NORDAU'S FIVE POINTS.

[REG. G.P.O. AS A NEWSPAPER.]

ESTABLISHED

FOR EVERY JEW

Two Pence.

AN ANGLO-JEWISH JOURNAL

WEDNESDAY, OCT. 8, 1919.—TISHRI 14, 5680.

London Jewish Hospital

STEPNEY GREEN, E. 1

A Banquet

WILL BE HELD IN

Celebration of the Opening of the London Jewish Hospital

AT THE

SAVOY HOTEL, W.

ON

TUESDAY, OCTOBER 28th, 1919

The Right Hon. Lord Rothschild

WILL PRESIDE.

TICKETS, £1 : 10 : 0 (INCLUSIVE OF WINES)

MAY BE OBTAINED FROM:

THE SECRETARY, 51a, Stepney Green, E, 1

JOHANNESBURG,
BARNATO BROS.,
KIMBERLEY.

TELEGRAPHIC ADDRESS,
"BARNATO, LONDON."

TELEPHONE Nº 1232 LONDON WALL.

109*A, Austin Friars,
Throgmorton Street,
London, **February** 26th 1919

E.C.

Dear Dr Levy,

I have just returned to town and find your letter awaiting me.

With regard to the proposed Jewish Hospital I have discussed the matter with my Co-trustees and we are all more or less against the scheme. We came to the conclusion that the establishment of such an Institution would be most unwise; and you may remember that this was the view I personally was inclined to take when we had an interview on the subject.

Yours faithfully,

Dr A. G. Levy,
2 Manchester Square,
W.

(XIX) *Letter from Jack Barnato Joel to Dr Goodman Levy that 'more or less' spelled out the end of any hope of support from the Barnato legacy.*
[University of Southampton Library Archives]

(XX) *It costs rather more to dine at the Savoy today.*
[Jewish World, 8 October 1919]

(XXI)   *The Festival Dinner held at the Savoy Hotel to celebrate the opening of the out-patient department of the Hospital, and the key presented to Lord Rothschild to commemorate the occasion.*
[Jewish World, 5 November 1919]

LONDON JEWISH HOSPITAL,

STEPNEY GREEN, E. 1.

THE Treasurer acknowledges with grateful thanks the following donations paid or notified on the occasion of the Festival Dinner of the London Jewish Hospital, on October 28th :—

Donor	£ s d
Abraham, B., Esq.	£10 10 0
Abrahams, Samuel, Esq.	10 10 0
Alexander, A., Esq.	1 1 0
Anonymous	1,000 0 0
Anonymous	1 10 0
Anonymous (to name a bed)	1,000 0 0
Barkoff, Mrs. R.	1 1 0
Barnett, Mrs. Louis	2 2 0
Barnett, Louis, Esq.	5 5 0
Bass, P., Esq.	10 10 0
Benjamin, M., Esq.	1 1 0
Berlin, S., Esq.	10 10 0
Berliner, I., Esq.	3 3 0
Birn, Mrs. S.	2 2 0
Birn, Moutie, Esq.	1 1 0
Black, T., Esq.	5 0 0
Bloomekoper, George, Esq.	5 5 0
Blumenthal, Mrs. J.	1 1 0
Blumenthal, J. H., Esq.	1 1 0
Botzman, B., Esq.	3 3 0
Brownstone, A., Esq.	10 10 0
Burnford, Dr. Julius	5 5 0
Chajes, H., Esq.	1 1 0
Charles, Albert, Esq. (yearly)	1 1 0
Charles, John, Esq. (yearly)	10 10 0
Charles, Joseph J., Esq. (yearly)	1 1 0
Cohen, Mrs. D. S.	1 1 0
Cohen, D. S., Esq.	1 1 0
Cohen, Mrs. Joseph	10 10 0
Cohen, Joseph, Esq.	10 10 0
Cohen, Mrs. P.	10 10 0
Cohen, Mrs. W.	2 2 0
Cohen, W., Esq.	3 3 0
Cohn, Mrs. Maurice	3 3 0
Cope, Mrs. Jane	10 10 0
Cowen, Isaac Morris, Esq.	5 5 0
Davids, Julius, Esq.	2 2 0
D.M.D.	10 0
Davis, A., Esq.	2 2 0
Davidson, Fred, Esq.	2 2 0
Davidson, Henry, Esq.	210 0 0
Deitsch, R., Esq.	5 5 0
Desser, Z., Esq.	10 10 0
Dimson, Mrs. R.	10 10 0
Dreyfus, Messrs. Louis & Co.	2 0 0
Elton, J., Esq.	2 0 0
Erson, Mr.	5 5 0
Finegold, C., Esq.	10 10 0
Fox, Mrs. Hilda	2 2 0
Frank, Harry, Esq.	10 10 0
Frank, Leo, Esq.	5 5 0
Freedlander, Henry, Esq.	10 10 0
Freedman, A., Esq.	10 10 0
Freedman, Mr. & Mrs. L.	2 2 0
Gee, Arthur, Esq.	2 2 0
Gilbert Family (in memory of Sophie Kohn)	500 0 0
Gold, Isaac, Esq.	100 0 0
Goldberg, Mr. & Mrs.	2 0 0
Goldrei, A., Esq.	5 5 0
Goldsmith, Mrs. Paula	2 2 0
Goldstein, Mrs. A.	1 1 0
Goldstein, A., Esq.	1 1 0
Goodman, Paul, Esq.	1 1 0
Green, Rev. A. A.	2 2 0
Greenberg, L. J., Esq.	2 12 6
Grew, Mrs. Paula	10 10 0
Gubbay, E. A., Esq.	50 0 0
Gutchman, Mr. and Mrs. J.	3 3 0
Halperin, Mrs. R.	1 1 0
Halperin, L. G., Esq.	10 10 0
Harris, Rev. and Mrs. J. S.	10 6
Hirschfield, Mrs. A.	10 10 0
Isaac, Bernard A., Esq.	2 2 0
Isner, M., Esq.	3 0 0
Jacob, Harry, Esq.	2 2 0
Jacobi, Mrs. Pauline	2 2 0
Jacobs, Daniel, Esq.	10 10 0
Josephat, Arnin, Esq.	3 3 0
Josephat, Mrs. Henrietta	2 2 0
Joseph, David, Esq.	2 2 0
Joseph, George, Esq.	2 2 0
Kaplan, I., Esq.	10 10 0
Katzman, Mrs. D.	2 12 6
Katzman, M., Esq.	2 12 6
Kiley, J. D., Esq., M.P.	10 10 0
Koransky, Mrs. J.	10 10 0
Koransky, M., Esq.	5 5 0
Kornblum, Mrs. R.	1 1 0
Kornblum, J., Esq.	2 2 0
Kosky, Mrs. Harry	10 10 0
Kutas, Mrs. E.	5 5 0
Lazarus, Mrs. L.	2 2 0
Lazarus, Leopold, Esq.	3 3 0
Levin, Mrs. A.	26 5 0
Levin, A., Esq.	26 5 0
Levy, Dr. and Mrs. A. G.	10 10 0
Levy, Mrs. Kitty	1 1 0
Levy, Sol, Esq.	10 10 0
Levy, William L., Esq.	5 0 0
Levy-Tebitt, Michael, Esq.	1 1 0
Lewis, Mrs. R.	10 10 0
Lighton, I., Esq.	10 10 0
Limberg, A., Esq.	3 0 0
Lipman, M., Esq.	2 2 0
Lloyd, Mrs. B.	10 10 0
Lloyds Bank, Ltd.	105 0 0
Loodmer, S., Esq.	5 5 0
Lyons, Louis, Esq. (yearly)	2 2 0
Mackrell, H. R., Esq.	1 1 0
Magasiner, Mrs. F. (yearly)	1 1 0
Mandel, Master L. J. (yearly)	2 2 0
Mesnitz, Mrs. H.	2 0 0
Michaelis, Max, Esq.	5 5 0
Miller, B., Esq.	10 10 0
Moser, Jacob, Esq.	5 5 0
Moses, Simon, Esq.	10 10 0
Myer, Morris, Esq.	5 5 0
Nathan, David, Esq.	10 10 0
Nathan, H. S., Esq.	5 5 0
Nathan, Mrs. L. H.	5 5 0
Nathan, M. J., Esq.	1 1 0
Newman, Bernard, Esq.	2 2 0
Newman, Morris, Esq. (yearly)	10 10 0
Nicoresti, Mr. and Mrs. J. Cofman	21 0 0
Oldak, Felix, Esq.	10 10 0
Prager, I., Esq.	25 0 0
Ring, Mrs. E.	10 6
Ring, E., Esq.	1 1 0
Salmon, Joseph, Esq. (Messrs. Cuff and Co., Ltd.) (yearly)	2 2 0
Samuels, Mrs. Dorothy	3 0 0
Sassoon, Mrs. F.	5 0 0
Sassoon, Mr. and Mrs. D.	2 0 0
Schalit, M., Esq.	100 0 0
Schen, Mrs. E. G.	2 2 0
Schlesinger, Richard, Esq.	5 5 0
Schon-Field, Mrs. Amalie	10 10 0
Schonberg, S., Esq.	50 0 0
Schonfield, Gustave, Esq.	10 10 0
Seligman, H. E., Esq.	10 10 0
Seligman, Isaac, Esq.	20 0 0
Seligman, Oscar, Esq.	5 5 0
Shire, N. M., Esq.	5 5 0
Silverstein, Mrs.	2 2 0
Silverstein, A., Esq.	3 3 0
Sollash, Mrs. I.	2 2 0
Sollash, I., Esq.	3 3 0
Sollash, Mrs. P.	2 2 0
Sollash, Philip, Esq.	10 10 0
Sollash, Miss Bessie	1 1 0
Solomons, J., Esq.	2 2 0
Somekh, S. S., Esq.	10 10 0
Szpigner, Dr. S. L.	1 0 0
Spiro, Mrs. L.	5 5 0
Spitzel, Victor, Esq.	10 10 0
Stern, H., Esq.	1 1 0
Stern, I., Esq.	1 1 0
Steele, A., Esq.	1 1 0
Strowe, Sydney, Esq.	110 10 0
Syder, L., Esq.	1 1 0
Tuck, Michael, Esq.	5 5 0
Tannenbaum, A., Esq.	2 2 0
Tarlo, Mrs. G.	5 5 0
Usiskin, S., Esq.	10 10 0
Vermont, Capt. J.	10 10 0
Vermont, Joseph Esq.	5 5 0
Vermont, Leon, Esq.	100 0 0
Walford, Lionel, Esq.	1 10 0
Warschawsky, Mrs. R.	10 10 0
Watson, J. L., Esq.	2 2 0
Weber, W., Esq.	1 1 0
Weinstein, J., Esq.	10 10 0
Weitzberg, Mrs. E.	2 2 0
Weitzberg, H., Esq.	1 1 0
Weitzberg, J., Esq.	2 2 0
Witte, Mrs. B.	5 5 0
Wolff, Henry, Esq. (in memory of his Mother and Father	50 0 0
Woolf, K., Esq.	10 10 0
Woolf, A. E. Mortimer, Esq., F.R.C.S.	5 5 0
Woolf, Mortimer, Esq.	5 5 0
Yahuda, Dr. A. S.	5 0 0
Zanarotsky, R. D., Esq.	10 10 0
Total	**£4,302 10 6**

The Secretary would be obliged if outstanding donations be sent direct to him at 51a, Stepney Green, E. 1.

(XXII) *List of donors at the Savoy Dinner. More was raised in one evening than the Association had collected in the previous three years. The Rothschild name had worked its magic.*

[Jewish World, 26 November 1919]

The London
Jewish Hospital
Before Nationalisation

THE HOSPITAL OPENS

The Out-patient Department Opens

At long last it was reported at the Annual Court of Governors held on 9 May 1919 that, some twelve years after the movement had started, the London Jewish Hospital was to open its doors in July, for out-patients only. Their doctors were being demobilised, but they required more to complete their staff. Guy's Hospital promised to admit any cases requiring indoor treatment. They were taking steps to build another floor, to provide a ward, a laboratory, and an efficient almoner's block, all of which would cost £40,000. A special vote of thanks was given to the *Jewish Chronicle* and the *Jewish World* for their support over the years. Those elected to office were, President, Isador Berliner; vice-presidents, Mrs A. Leibster and Messrs J. L. Berman, E. B. Kapp and H. Wolff; Treasurer, Dr A. Gaster.

The consecration of the out-patient department took place on Sunday, 13 July. At the ceremony, the Haham took the opportunity to issue a warning, 'Beware of the Rich!':[1]

The addition of rich subscriptions, beneficial as otherwise it is inasmuch as it may quicken the work, harbours a danger against which I must raise a voice of warning. It may slacken the enthusiasm of the poorer subscribers, it may introduce again a spirit of dependence on the rich which, in the long run, may prove a very serious check on the prosperity of the hospital. The greatness and beauty of the Institute lies in its popular origin, in the sustained personal interest which the larger masses are taking in its welfare. When rich men come on to the scene, often a kind of oligarchy is established, and the fear of losing a rich subscription has often jeopardised the best interests of a Jewish institution. With the humbler subscriber the danger cannot arise. He will not claim any special rights. He will not insist on carrying out his views; his own individuality counts practically for nothing. It is all merged in the greater purpose of keeping up the hospital, school or other charitable institute.

It is interesting to speculate why the Haham chose this moment to issue this warning. He knew the Cousinhood were capable of passing seamlessly from opposition to support, and of taking over the reins of control. Was he concerned because such a takeover had happened in the past, as with the Home for Aged Jews and the Jews' Temporary Shelter? Was he in possession of information that pointed towards its happening with the Hospital? Was it connected in any way with the meeting of 27 January at the home of Mr Cohn?

Understandable as it was for the Haham to point to these 'dangers', and unwilling as he must have been to see the fruits of the pioneers taken out of their hands, it is difficult to agree with him. The writing was clearly on the wall for voluntary hospitals, the financially strongest of which were finding the task of raising sufficient funds to maintain their standards almost beyond them. Hospital subscriptions from the middle classes had declined, and wartime inflation had increased costs considerably. The *Jewish Chronicle* was probably being much more realistic in its editorial of 18 July when it again called on the rich to assist.

Over the years of struggle the view had been expressed by many of the promoters of the scheme, particularly by Berliner, that although the rich had held back, they would join in once the hospital was open. Whether they would or not, time would tell.

On 2 October 1919, the *Jewish Chronicle* carried an advertisement for a banquet to be held at the Savoy Hotel in the Strand on Tuesday, 28 October 1919, to celebrate the opening of the London Jewish Hospital.[2] Tickets were priced at £1.10.0 (inclusive of wines). 'The Right Honourable Lord Rothschild will preside'. How the wheel had turned!

The *Jewish Chronicle* approved:

Next Sunday the Jewish Hospital is to be formally opened and the function is to be followed by a banquet on the following Tuesday. On both occasions the chief part is to be taken by Lord Rothschild, a fact to be particularly welcomed, having regard to the opposition to the Hospital that was once manifested in those circles in the community to which he pre-eminently belongs. We hope that the imprimatur now to be given the institution by Lord Rothschild will be appreciated and copied elsewhere. The Hospital has come to stay. But it will need every assistance if it is to do its work in a manner which will be creditable to the Jewish name, and although there was a touch almost of the heroic in the way in which the poor built it brick by brick, there will be a call on all of us, rich and poor, to keep it going in a worthy manner.

At the ceremony at the Hospital Lord Rothschild, who had been elected a vice-president, was greeted with loud cheers. The speakers were Rothschild, Joseph Hertz, the Chief Rabbi who had not previously sat on their platform, J. Kiley the M.P. for Stepney, and Dr Goodman Levy.

The *Jewish Chronicle*'s report of the banquet was headlined 'A notable gathering', and described the hospital enterprise as a labour of love. In proposing the toast 'Success to the Hospital', Lord Rothschild said the Hospital deserved to succeed, because while the great bulk of charitable institutions owed their inception and culmination to one man, or a few men, the London Jewish Hospital owed its inception and culmination to the efforts, exertions, and sacrifices of the great mass of the Jewish people of the metropolis. It was essentially a movement started by the people for the people.

Berliner was given a heartfelt welcome. He said an early meeting of the movement twelve years earlier had also been held at the Savoy Hotel, but that was the Savoy Hotel near the Morgan Street market in the East End. Dr Burnford emphasised that the Hospital would not interfere with the work of the local general practitioners, and it would not countenance any abuse of its facilities. The constant emphasis that was placed on this suggests that the general practitioners must have expressed concern that they might lose to the Hospital out-patient department those who could well afford to pay a doctor privately.

The two events provided the opportunity for Greenberg to say what he really felt about those leaders of the community who had opposed the movement. His editorial[3] reads as though he was releasing pent-up feelings he had contained for years, and he used abrasive and abusive language of the kind seldom seen in newspapers today. He commented on the shameful absence of those who purported to lead the community; Lord Rothschild was alone. Apart from the Chief Rabbi and Rev A A Green, of the ministry there were none:

> The Hospital movement, which began in the humblest way was frowned upon and denounced by men who purported to lead the community. They not only cold-shouldered the idea; they ridiculed it. They jeered at the patient efforts of these humbler folk. They exhausted their vocabulary of abuse, describing the promoters of the Hospital as either *meshugga* or endowed with a double dose of Jewish *chutspa*. They decried them as anxious to maintain an 'alien' spirit between Jews and non-Jews, and thus as disloyal segregants. The movement was tabooed as retrograde, as foolish, as impracticable, as everything it ought not to be and nothing that it should.

> We were assured that no one would give any money to the scheme – at least no one who had any money. That has proved to a large extent to be true. The rich members of the community have closed their pockets, with their hearts, and both are being but gradually released. But those who banked their opinions on this cash deficit, forgot that twelve pennies from twelve persons are precisely of the same financial value as one shilling from one man – and are of infinitely more moral worth. And the pence of the many have been substituted for the pounds of the few. It has been a lesson of which the wise should take timely note, this magnificent revolt of the Jewish proletariat against the Jewish plutocracy, of Jewish Jews in support of an essentially Jewish institution.

He also used the occasion to make a wider point. Just six days before the banquet Parliament was debating an Aliens' Bill, and some speakers accused

Russian immigrant Jews of fostering vice and crime, being deficient in cleanliness, liable to introduce disease into the country, and gravely interfering with Christian observance. Greenberg commented:

> Who and what are the men and women who have valiantly carried through this Hospital Scheme? They are just the men and women who are at this very moment being pilloried and maligned in Parliament and in the press as undesirable aliens; they are the denizens of the East End who are being paraded as an element detrimental, if not dangerous, to the country – men and women for whom the gentlemen of England can find no prescription except 'Deport the lot!' Yet in truth it is these men and women, the poorest of the poor of them, who with the earnings of their sweat and their blood, have succeeded in making the beginnings of a great healing palace, which will be Jewish, but which in the beneficent work it does, will know no discrimination in respect to creed, or faith, or race, and to the portals of which the only 'open sesame' will be a need of the healing art.

> It was men and women, alien Jews and Jewesses from the East End, who formed some seventy-five or eighty per cent of the company at the banquet on Tuesday evening. It would have been good if some of those English gentlemen from the House of Commons further down the Embankment could have come and seen the men and women they are so fond of maligning, there assembled – if they could have observed the lusty enthusiasm with which these 'disoloyal' 'Bolshevist' East End alien Jews sang *God Save the King*; could have noted their personal appearance, their dress, their behaviour and their conduct – as faultless and commendable as that of any gathering in any banqueting hall in the West End of the town. The sight must have shamed them for the outrageous libels which some of these men have been so recklessly uttering in the House of Commons these last few days.

The Chief Rabbi, Dr Joseph Hertz, said the Hospital was a symbol of the release of the poorer Jews from the bonds of benificence.

The first list of donations at the dinner totalled £4,302.10.6d. This equalled in one evening the amount the LJHA had previously collected in three years. The Rothschild name had already worked its magic.

The first tablet unveiled in the Waiting Room of the out-patient department was in memory of Pioneer Samuel Abrahams, the son of Mr and Mrs John Abrahams of Whitechapel Road, who was killed in action on 27 May 1918.

The In-patient Department Opens

At the Annual Court of Governors, (subscribers of one guinea or more per annum), held on 11 April 1920 at Anderton's Hotel, Fleet Street. Goodman Levy reported that the total income in 1919 had been £10,300, no less than £8,000 of which had been received in the last six months of the year. The Hospital out-patient department was open four mornings and five afternoons a week and patients were attending at the rate of 600 per week. No charge was made, but patients were invited to contribute towards the Hospital's funds as far as possible to help pay for drugs and dressings. The existing general policy of other London hospitals suggested that in the near future the advisability of a compulsory charge might have to be considered.

The governors planned to establish two in-patient wards. Premises for additional nursing staff were also needed, but lack of funds had hampered progress. Despite this, instructions were given to the contractors to start on the first floor of the Hospital immediately work on the ground floor was completed.

By the time of the fourteenth Annual General Meeting, held in April 1921, the financial status of the Hospital within the Jewish community ranked second only to the Jewish Board of Guardians. Close ties were soon cemented with the Board and with the Invalid Children's Aid Association; the District Nurses' Association; East London and Hackney Branches for Home Nursing; the Infant Welfare Centres for home visiting, Jewish ministers who obtained Hospital Sunday Fund grants; and the LCC School Care Committee for milk and dental treatment.

The culmination of all their work came when the in-patient department was consecrated and officially opened on Sunday, 11 December 1921 by the Chief Rabbi, the Haham, and Lord Rothschild.[4] There were twenty-one beds in two medical wards, one male and one female, and four cots. Surgical wards had been built, but remained unoccupied pending the construction of an operating theatre for major operations, and the building of housing accommodation for the extra nursing and domestic staff who would be required.

Berliner said that money alone could not have built the hospital. It had needed unbounded enthusiasm. The meeting in the kitchen of the house in Sydney Street had led to its ultimate goal.

Payment by Patients

Except in cases of emergency, in-patients required, as was the case in most voluntary hospitals, to have a subscriber's letter of recommendation before being admitted (see illustration XLIV). Donors to the Hospital of £10 in a year were entitled to recommend one patient in the year in which the donation was made; donors of £30 were entitled to recommend one patient annually, and executors of a person making a bequest of £100 or more could also recommend one patient annually. Annual subscribers of two guineas could recommend one patient a year. Many donors gave their ration of letters to charity organisations such as the Jewish Board of Guardians or to ministers, who then distributed them. So great was the congestion at the Hospital that in 1923 letters of recommendation were introduced for out-patients too, and that remained a requirement until 1928.[5]

In 1913, Sir William Osler, the Regius Professor of Medicine at Oxford, had commented on the prospect of the voluntary system being able to maintain its 'free of charge' policy. He bluntly told his audience of hospital administrators and supporters, 'Give it up; it is antiquated, out-of-date, and it is not going to continue. Make up your minds that you must accept the principle of taking pay from patients'. An increasing number of hospitals began to charge patients who could afford to pay, and gradually charges were introduced at the London Jewish Hospital too. Patients given extract of malt and cod liver oil paid twopence to cover the cost of the container, and dental patients had to cover the cost of anaesthetics. A charge was imposed of one penny per medicine bottle, rising to threepence according to size, and patients were responsible for supplying their own tea, sugar and butter. In 1921, an out-patient charge of sixpence per visit was introduced.[6]

An in-patient's financial position was assessed by the almoner, and an appropriate contribution asked for, although the House Committee emphasised that she should accept any lesser amount offered by the patient or his family, being careful not to convey the impression that treatment would be withheld unless the payment assessed by her was paid. She could always raise the matter of a higher contribution after the treatment was completed.

Additions to the medical staff included Leopold Mandel as assistant physician, A. E. Mortimer Woolf assistant surgeon, and Harold Chapple as gynaecologist. Nathan Jacobowicz was replaced as Secretary by Morris Stephany. All the medical staff were Jewish, with the exception of a Sister in Charge, and a single exception in the Honorary Visiting Staff, the surgeon E. C. Hughes. Almost all the remaining staff, including the nurses, dispensers, and porters could speak Yiddish.

From the outset, both Jewish and non-Jewish patients were treated, thus fulfilling a promise the organisers had made throughout their campaign. By 1926, 40% of out-patients were non-Jewish. The percentage of non-Jewish in-patients varied between 20% and 35%, but after World War II the non-Jewish cases increased, and the London Jewish Hospital found itself in the position of the German Hospital – catering mainly for a class other than that for which it was primarily founded.

A Ladies' Aid Association was formed under the presidency of Mrs J. H. Hertz, the Chief Rabbi's wife, and the chairmanship of Mrs J. Burnford, the wife of the Hospital's honorary physician. Greenberg's wife, Florence, was its secretary. Dora Shuster, who had been a collector when a child, joined the Committee and was to serve the Hospital for many years, latterly as Lady Almoner. Amongst other comforts, the Aid Association supplied one daily and two weekly Yiddish papers. In co-operation with the branches, the Association formed an After-Care Committee to assist the Lady Almoner in arranging for convalescent treatment and providing extra nourishment, such as eggs and milk; paying for dentures and surgical instruments for necessitous patients; and, where necessary, paying taxi fares for patients leaving hospital. They laid on special teas at Chanukah and Purim. The money used for these purposes came from a fund known as the 'Leah Gaster Fund'. The Association also provided surgical aid letters, grocery tickets, and bread, meat and coal tickets for disbursement by the Lady Almoner.

Once the London Jewish Hospital was fully operational it fell into line with other voluntary hospitals, having to face the same realities – the increasing cost of medical care, the increased demand for it, and the difficulty of raising funds. It had the added disadvantage of beginning its life without a Foundation Fund. As Viscount Knutsford had forewarned them, they had to confine their attention to those they could cure. It became strictly an acute hospital. Those suffering from incurable diseases, chronic complaints, mental diseases, infectious fevers, venereal diseases, or those requiring merely rest, or who would otherwise be more suitably treated at a Poor Law institution, were not admitted. Visiting hours were as restricted as those in the general hospitals, Wednesdays from 3–4 and Saturdays 3–4.30.

Goodman Levy gradually began to assume greater administrative control. He was chairman of the Council of Management, of the House Committee, and of the Building Sub-Committee, in addition to being chairman of the West London Branch Committee. Both he and Berliner regularly attended the Hospital, almost on a daily basis, but it was Goodman Levy who was coming to the fore.

Death of Isador Berliner

Berliner was not in the best of health. He and his wife were bronchitis sufferers, and during the winter months spent part of their time in Nice or Monte Carlo. This they could now afford, for Berliner had long since given up his barber shop. In 1914, he opened what became a very successful menswear business at 181 Commercial Road under the trading name of I. Berliner & Son. The family lived in the extensive premises above the shop, which included a large drawing room that sported splendid chandeliers, much to the wonderment of their grandchildren. It was expensively furnished. Berliner's improved circumstances were rarely mentioned publicly – he was still referred to as 'an East End barber'.

He more and more confined himself to liaison with the branch committees, and for a short time chaired the Joint Branches Committee,[7] and organised sub-committees dealing with collecting boxes and collections at weddings, barmitzvahs, Brith Melah, and other functions. Due to his ill-health, he passed over the chairmanship of this committee to Mr I. M. Shocket.

Isidor Berliner died in December 1925, aged fifty-four. The funeral cortege left from 181 Commercial Road. The street was lined with hundreds, if not thousands, of his friends and those who had benefitted from the work of the Hospital he had done so much to establish. It passed along Commercial Road to Philpott Street and then through to Whitechapel, along Mile End Road and on to Stepney Green. There it stopped close to the steps of the Hospital on which all the doctors, nurses and other staff were standing to see him off. After two or three minutes silence, the hearse moved on and took him to his final resting place at Marlow Road Cemetery, East Ham where he is buried alongside his wife.[8]

The *Jewish Chronicle* described him[9] as a humble man carrying on a humble vocation who managed to carve for himself an enduring monument of which any prince might be proud. Tributes portrayed him as 'a benefactor of his people', enjoying 'profound common sense', 'largeness of heart, perseverance and honesty of purpose', 'pride of race', and 'quiet dignity'. He was a man who 'lived for the Hospital', had a 'cheery optimism when faced by disappointment', was 'an inspiration to all his co-workers', and had 'sterling integrity', 'boundless charity', and a 'charming personality'. The *Jewish World*[10] said that the Hospital was one of the most remarkable monuments to the memory of a humble trader that it could recall, and 'all the Jewish Hospital is, all the good, both direct and indirect, it is doing or is going to do, is due to the steadfast kind heartedness of Mr Berliner'. To his family he was a generous man, never too busy to help a poor person. Every Sunday he would 'receive' visitors between 1–3 coming to him for help. His wife was for ever calling him in for his meal, but he kept her waiting until he had dealt with the last visitor. Of rare spirit, with zeal and courage, he was the undoubted catalyst for the movement. His was, by any test, a remarkable achievement.

His son, Victor, a well-known and respected boxing promoter, carried on his work at the hospital, and remained an active member of the Council of Management and many of its committees until his death in 1949. The Berliner family connection had spread over forty years. It was a fitting tribute to Berliner that the man considered to be worthy of succeeding him as President was Viscount Erleigh, later the Marquis of Reading.[11]

Three more storeys were needed to complete the front block as originally designed. The out-patient department was in urgent need of expansion and forty extra beds were required, including seven for a separate children's ward. The main kitchen and the domestic offices were unsatisfactorily placed in the small basement of an adjoining house that was used as a Nurses' Home. Additional land was purchased, and in all £25,000 was needed to make essential improvements. In 1926 a special appeal for that sum was made. Bernhard Baron, the tobacco philanthropist, responded by giving £10,000.[12]

Greenberg took the opportunity to continue his bombardment of the consciences of those of the rich who still did not support the Hospital as he thought they should. Shortly before a fund-raising dinner held at the Savoy Hotel on 29 November he wrote In the *Jewish Chronicle*:[13]

So the Hospital now wants the sum of £25,000. It is a comparatively trifling amount – I mean, of course, when compared with the value that is to be given for it. It is a long way from that little meeting in the little room in the little basement in an East End Street, to a banquet presided over by a Rothschild, attended by an ex-prime minister – for Mr Lloyd George has intimated his intention of being present – followed, naturally they follow, by the pluto-aristocracy of the community. The part these are called upon to perform for the institution is child's play when compared with what those poor people did – poor, I would again stress, in material gifts. They had to work and labour and strive and contrive for pennies and halfpennies and farthings, to canvass from house to house, night after night, in storm, in rain, in tempest or when the atmosphere in the alleys and byways they visited was well-nigh asphyxiating.

The work which the materially wealthy who are to attend this Dinner are called upon to do is for them as easy as kiss your hand. They have merely to take the example of the gentleman who is presiding at the meeting, [James de Rothschild], or of that grand old philanthropist Mr Bernhard Baron, and write out their cheques for large amounts they will never miss. If just a few give, not what they feel bound to give, but as much as they ought to wish to give, then that poor man's dream of twenty years ago will be fulfilled. The poor man's dream has now become the rich man's opportunity. He will surely embrace it with avidity if only to compensate for the discouragement the dream met with by, (as a whole), the class to whom the rich belong, and its neglect of the Hospital ever since.

There were 500 guests at the dinner, including the Chief Rabbi, Lord Rothschild, Bernhard Baron, Sir Robert Waley Cohen, Viscount Erleigh, Sir Elly Kadoorie, Mr Lloyd George, and the Marquis of Reading. More than £20,000 was raised, the largest donations being from J. B. Joel (£525) and the Hon Mrs N. Rothschild (£500). The list of donors showed that almost all lived either in the

West End or North West London; only a very small proportion of the total raised emanated from East Enders (see illustration XXII). A children's ward opened in March 1927, and the remaining extension in 1928.

Income from investments, upon which many hospitals relied for a considerable part of their stable income, provided only 1% of the annual expenditure of the London Jewish Hospital; patients' contributions secured 25%; and Central Funds 12%. This left 62% to be collected every year in the form of subscriptions, donations, and the proceeds of functions organised by the Branches. The Hospital's income from subscriptions and donations during the period 1920–1928 was:

	Annual Subscriptons	Donations
1920	833	5429
1921	879	8367
1922	885	4488
1923	892	7639
1924	1059	8709
1925	1196	6131
1926	1172	3642
1927	1686	6680
1928	2064	7045

Over the same period, annual receipts averaged £1,300 from box collections; £1,000 from cinema performances; £1,200 from in-patients, rising to £1,715 by 1928; £1,200 from out-patients; and payment for medicine bottles £100.

Generally the Hospital was run on sound financial principles, and until the mid-1930s kept its expenditure in line with its income. Contrary to the forecasts of its opponents, the Hospital received contributions from the three main hospital funds, the King's Fund, the Hospital Saturday Fund and the Hospital Sunday Fund. Also, from 1927, it obtained an increasing income from its arrangement with the Hospital Savings Association.

However, the collection of so much of its income in small amounts meant administration costs were higher than average. This, plus duplicate kitchens and utensils for milk and meat, and the higher cost of kosher basic foods, (for example kosher poultry was 30% dearer, and kosher milk was 4d per gallon dearer than non-kosher), led, by 1938, to an accumulated deficit of £4,000.

The number of beds, originally 25, was increased to 108 by 1930. During the 1930s, an average of 1,500 in-patients were admitted each year, and out-patient visits rose from 44,264 in 1925 to 83,152 in 1935. The cost of treating patients in

1935, including the cost of provisions, surgery, dispensary, salaries, wages, administration, establishment renewals and repairs, was an average of 1/8d per visit by out-patients, and £3.50 per week for in-patients.

The prevailing economic depression held up further developments, but attention became focussed on the Nurses' Home which, in 1935, was described as 'a disgrace'. The target this time was £40,000, successfully raised. The foundation stone was laid by the Marchioness of Reading in July 1938, and the Nurses' Home was opened by Mrs James de Rothschild in April 1939.

Facilities at the London Jewish Hospital, comparing like with like, were as good as non-Jewish hospitals, even though there were snags about the building because it had been built piecemeal. Dr Ian Gordon, who joined the staff in 1932, said that it was a busy hospital, and the practice was good and varied with a great deal of acute medicine and acute surgery. Because the patients had something in common with the doctors they were not frightened by them. 'In non-Jewish hospitals', said Gordon, 'Jewish patients were not exactly frightened, but inhibited perhaps. At the London Jewish Hospital the patients were not in the slightest inhibited', and this led to a congenial atmosphere on the wards.

THE HOSPITAL IN THE 1920s
AND 1930s

Prior to the outbreak of World War II, the London Jewish Hospital was a good example of the best work that could be done by a local hospital closely involved with the community it served. Dr Gordon said it had 'a first class, really tip top team of physicians and surgeons'. The quality of the dedicated medical staff and consultants it was able to attract was one of its undoubted strengths. The variety of their experience, at the London Jewish Hospital and at the other hospitals they served, provided a solid base upon which the London Jewish Hospital could prosper.

The Jewish medical community in London in the 1930s, very much smaller in numbers than it is now, was well knit, aided in this by the existence of the London Jewish Medical Society.[1] Originally called the London Jewish Hospital Medical Society, it was established on 8 October 1928 and was the brainchild of Maurice Sorsby (previously Sourasky), then an assistant consultant surgeon in the ear, nose and throat department. A young, dynamic immigrant, ardently embracing Zionist and socialist ideals, a scion of a prominent and respected East End family wholly committed to the Jewish cause, he persuaded the restrained, assimilated Goodman Levy, whose links with Jewry were almost wholly philanthropic, that a medical society would enhance the prestige of the Hospital; would spread information about the good work carried on there; and thereby attract wider support, professional, and possibly financial, for its development.

Goodman Levy was elected President and Dr Julius Burnford Vice-President. Arnold Sorsby, Louis Forman, Noah Pines and S. I. Levy were among the first members of council. Subsequent Presidents included Burnford, Dr Leopold Mandel, who was a consultant paediatrician to the Hospital from 1919 until after World War II; Maurice Sorsby, Harold Kisch, Dr Eder, Arnold Sorsby, Harold Levy, Dr Bethel Solomons, S. I. Levy, Samson Wright, Samuel Dimson, Professor John Yudkin, Ian Gordon, and A. Radcliffe. In 1955, Dr Max Sorsby became the first general practitioner to be elected as President, and he was followed by fellow general practitioners Dr Sammy Sacks, Dr Hannah Billig, and Dr Laurence Phillips. An annual dinner was introduced in 1929, held until 1939 at the Trocadero, Piccadilly Circus, and an annual oration instituted and delivered over the years by distinguished figures eminent in their branch of medicine. Important symposiums were arranged on such subjects as *Diseases of the Jews*.[2]

Sorsby believed the Society could provide a forum in which Jewish doctors could meet and discuss professional matters in an atmosphere free of self-consciousness. Jewish general practitioners spoke amongst themselves; the reputation of the Jewish consultants they admired quickly became known, and private work flowed to them.

Gordon said that Jewish doctors were attracted to the Hospital not only because it was a good hospital, but also because many faced discrimination after qualification. In the 1920s, 1930s, and even into the 1940s, a young Jewish doctor had to be very determined to obtain a satisfactory post. His usual options were to go straight into general practice, or take a position in a comparatively small, obscure hospital that had difficulty in attracting candidates. The London Jewish Hospital presented an alternative.

Many felt that anti-Semitism was one cause for this, and some found success only after they had anglicised their names. Mr Anthony Radcliffe, the eminent ear nose and throat surgeon, and later a distinguished consultant at the London Jewish Hospital, saw an advertisement in 1938 for a position at the Royal National E.N.T. Hospital in Golden Square, and obtained the post after changing his name from Rakoff to Ratcliffe on the suggestion of a non-Jewish governor of the Hospital. Dr Joseph Jacob, who was house surgeon and then house physician at the London Jewish Hospital in 1956–7, said that even then there was a great deal of prejudice in the teaching hospitals when it came to appointments.

There was also a certain amount of resistance to appointing Jews to senior appointments. Gordon considered it was not anti-semitism as a positive attitude, rather as a negative one. For those given the task of making appointments it was one thing to appoint a junior person, another to appoint someone who would be your colleague. 'You want as your colleague someone who is a peer rather than someone who is of a different species, and Jews were regarded by many as a different species. I was conscious of the fact that, all things being equal, if a Jew and a non-Jew applied, there was an element that would favour the non-Jew rather than the Jew, because he was an unknown quantity'.

The problem was not confined to England. Dr Maurice Fishberg, writing in the *Jewish World* in October 1917, said for more than one hundred years it had been very difficult for Jewish medical graduates to enter a general hospital in New York as an interne, and the rule still held good, though there had been many exceptions in more recent years. An oral examination followed the written one. The former was known to consist more in 'sizing up' the candidate for appointment than in testing his knowledge and attainments, and it was at that stage that many Jewish doctors failed. It was because of this that so many Jewish doctors in America sought and found positions in the Jewish hospitals. Prejudice against Jewish doctors in European hospitals has been well documented.

In England, class was another barrier, and not only for the Jewish candidate. Certain hospitals were known for the public school and Oxbridge backgrounds of their resident staff and consultants; inbreeding was the rule, and applicants from outside the circle could encounter difficulties. Jewish doctors particularly suffered from this since a much higher proportion of Jewish medical students came from a working class background than was the case generally.

It was the generation of London's Jewish children born between 1900 and 1925 who first considered entering the professions in any numbers. Dr Gordon, who was born in 1906, told the author that when he discussed the possibility of his studying to become a doctor with his parents they thought it was just a pipe-dream, but the idea that it was a possibility gradually grew on them.

Isaac (known as Ian) Gordon, the son of immigrants, was typical of several of the eighteen doctors[3] who served the London Jewish Hospital before and after it was absorbed into the National Health Service. His parents, Mark and Minnie, were born in Gombin and Zychlin respectively, *shtetls* near Warsaw in Poland. They had eight children, five of whom were born in Poland. As was the usual pattern of the time, Mark, who was orthodox, and was a woollen merchant, came to London in 1902, at the age of thirty-five, leaving his wife and five children behind. They followed in 1905.

Ian was born the following year, and two sisters came after him. The family of ten lived at 21 Princelet Street, Spitalfields in the heart of the Jewish East End until 1919; they then began the trail of the more successful Jewish East Enders to Stoke Newington, Stamford Hill and Golders Green. At home both English and Yiddish were spoken, and Gordon's teacher in religious studies taught in Yiddish, so that Gordon became fluent in the language. He was educated at Deal Street School and Whitechapel Foundation School at both of which the majority of children were Jewish. He had ambitions to be a doctor from an early age, and as his father was by now doing quite well in his business and could afford the fees both at Whitechapel Foundation and later at medical college, Gordon was encouraged to follow his ambition. Several of his fellow students at Whitechapel Foundation, mostly the children of tailors, cabinet makers and similar occupations, also went on to become doctors, including his contemporaries Sam Dimson, (later a colleague at the London Jewish Hospital), Michael Cremer, the distinguished consultant neurologist at the Middlesex Hospital, and Jack Secular a paedetrician at Central Middlesex Hospital.

Gordon had pre-medical studies at King's College, London, starting at the early age of sixteen. After King's, he was accepted for training at Bart's, though he was aware that ahead would be the greater problem of obtaining a hospital position after qualification. He spent almost his whole career at the London Jewish Hospital. A sister there described him as very caring and very religious.

Israel Prieskel, a surgeon, was born in 1907 in Vilkomir, Lithuania, one of four children. His father, Hirsch Woolf, was a diamond merchant. The family moved to Paris in 1912 and stayed there until 1914 when they moved to London. Israel spoke French and Yiddish at home, and was learned in the Talmud. In London, the Prieskel family lived in Clapton, and he attended Hackney Downs School (Grocers) before going on to Bart's. An excellent diagnostician, his tombstone inscription describes him as a physician and a scholar. He knew everything about the Hospital, and everybody in it.

Another with an unusual background was Dr Noah Pines. He was born in Russia in 1883, and qualified as an ophthalmic surgeon in Kiev. He served as a Lieutenant-Colonel medical officer in the Ulan regiment in the Tsarist army and was highly decorated for bravery. His wife, whom he met at the front, was the first woman doctor to be employed by the Orzay, a Jewish self-help organisation formed to combat a wave of typhoid and cholera in the Ukraine. When the Russian army collapsed they started a clinic, Noah acting as surgeon and his wife as the anaesthetist, in what was by then a part of Poland being fought over by the communists and the White Russians. For a time Dr Pines was imprisoned by the communists. He came to England alone in 1920, being one of the first Russian doctors to reach England after the Revolution. He lived in the East End in a small room, worked extremely hard, and re-qualified.

He sent for his family, and they lived at 41 Philpot Street, just behind the London Hospital and close to the Medical Mission, and there he stayed for the rest of his life. His three children all became doctors, and he was so proud of their achievements that he put up another brass plate on the door each time one qualified, so that eventually there were five plates, including one for his wife. She found learning English very difficult, and Russian was spoken at home; even his two English-born sons became fluent in Russian. He practised as a general practitioner in the East End for many years, and was consultant ophthalmic surgeon to the London Jewish Hospital in the 1930s and 1940s.

He ran a single-handed general practice, walked everywhere as he did not have a car, and to the amusement and delight of his children installed a screechy whistle by his bed attached to a pipe that led to his front door. Those in need of a doctor at night would have someone blow on the whistle, wake Dr Pines, give him the name and address of the patient, and he would rush to the house. Most of his local patients were Russian-born and were Yiddish speakers, but he was also popular with many of the Russian 'aristocracy' who had left Russia and lived in other parts of London. His daughter Dinora recalled[4] being brought into the surgery to meet princesses, expecting to find beautiful young women wearing tiaras, and being disappointed to be confronted with plainly-dressed elderly ladies. He was the official doctor to the Yiddish Theatre, which brought a colourful crowd to his surgery, and the ballet dancer Pavlova was one of his patients.

During World War II he was very active in the blitz, helping Mrs Lionel de Rothschild who was the local Commandant of the St John's ambulance Brigade, accompanying her on her nightly rounds of the shelters in the Whitechapel area. A firm supporter of the London Jewish Medical Society, he retained his strong Russian accent to the end; 'but it never deterred him from having his say. The more eloquent he waxed the more marked his accent became, till he sometimes verged on the incomprehensible to the bewildered delight of his hearers'.[5] Altogether he had followed a career path most unusual for a London hospital consultant of his time. Indeed, none of the above three could be considered to have enjoyed the usual background of a medical student of the day.

David Nunes Nabarro [1874–1958] came from a more established anglicised background, and was appointed to the staff even before the Hospital opened its doors in 1919. The son of a merchant, he was educated at Owen's School, University College London, and University College Hospital. Throughout his training he was a prize and scholarship winner. He was house physician at University College Hospital and a ship's surgeon before returning to University College Hospital as assistant professor of pathology. He also held the appointment of pathologist to the Evalina Hospital for Sick Children for some years. From 1912 to 1939 he was clinical pathologist to the Great Ormond Street Hospital for Sick Children, and for twenty years from 1908 scientific assistant in pathology in the University of London. Modest and retiring, he combined his work as consultant at the London Jewish Hospital with being for a time president of the London Jewish Hospital Medical Society.

Harold Albert Kisch [1880–1959], who was appointed to the London Jewish Hospital in 1915 came from a medical background; his father was in general practice for many years in Sutherland Avenue, Maida Vale, and his grandfather was an obstetric surgeon. He was educated at the City of London School and St Thomas's where he qualified in 1904. He was a prize winner, and then held house appointments at Brompton Hospital and St Thomas's. During the First World War he served with the Royal Army Medical Corps, much of the time in the Eastern Mediterranean.

After the war he was appointed assistant surgeon, and then surgeon, to the Central London Throat Nose and Ear Hospital where he gave devoted service for over forty years. He was also for many years surgeon in charge of the ear, nose and throat department of University College Hospital, and consultant to the London Jewish Hospital, the School for Deaf Children, and the Concert Artistes' Association. He took a keen interest in postgraduate teaching and impressed upon his students the value of a sound training and general experience before specialisation. A forceful personality, with a progressive outlook, he was blunt and outspoken, but beneath the gruff exterior kind and considerate.

Julius Meyer Burnford [1878–1972] was a stalwart of the London Jewish Hospital from 1915 to the late 1960s, serving on its Council of Management for many years. He had a wider experience and knowledge of its history, ambitions and faults than perhaps anyone else. Born in Manchester, and educated at Owen's College where he had an outstanding career, winning three scholarships, he was appointed assistant pathologist at Westminster Hospital but spent most of his life as physician to the West London Hospital and Putney Hospital, and as senior physician to the London Jewish Hospital. Before coming to the London Jewish he had seen service in both the Boer War, in which he was wounded in the foot by a rifle bullet (he said it was because 'the damned fools gave me a white horse to ride'), and World War I as a medical officer in Belgium, Gallipoli, Salonica and Mesopotamia. Kindly and helpful to those he liked, he was nonetheless a firm disciplinarian, with himself as well as others, and could be a little difficult at times.

Aaron Harold Levy [1875–1977] was educated at the Catholic Academy, Montreal, where he was a gold medalist, and trained at McGill University. He came to London and entered Guy's where he qualified, and in 1919 was the first ophthalmic surgeon to be appointed to the London Jewish Hospital. He held similar positions at Willesden General Hospital, Central London Ophthalmic Hospital and Putney General Hospital. He was also ophthalmic surgeon to Hayes Industrial School, (the Jewish Approved School), the Home for Aged Jews, the Jewish Blind Society, and St Monica's Hospital for Children. For twenty-five years he was managing director of the British Journal of Ophthalmology. He served in the Royal Army Medical Corps during the war. Sound and competent, he was beloved by his patients and admired and respected by his colleagues. Very active in Jewish circles, he was a member of the Jewish Board of Deputies and President of the Jewish Health Organisation. He died at the age of 101.

Harold Chapple, the gynaecologist at the Hospital during the 1920s and 1930s, was educated at Cambridge and Guy's where he was obstetric surgeon. He was also a consultant gynaecologist at St John's Hospital, Lewisham. He served in the R.A.M.C. during World War I.

Albert Davis (born 4 January 1904), a gynaecologist, was the youngest Hunterian Professor at the Royal College of Surgeons since Hunter himself. He had trained at Manchester Infirmary, Guy's and the Middlesex Hospitals, and went to Vienna, regarded as a leading medical centre. However, by the time he arrived, their thirteen Jewish professors had been dismissed, and its reputation had fallen. Back in London, he applied for the position of registrar at the Middlesex Hospital and reached the short list of two. While they were awaiting their interviews, the other applicant, who had been a house surgeon at the Hospital, suddenly burst into tears. He said his wife was pregnant, and he desperately needed the job. Davis walked out and did not attend his interview.

Instead, he joined the London Jewish Hospital as an assistant to Elsie Landau, and was later appointed a consultant at King's College Hospital, St Giles' Hospital, and the Bearsted Hospital. He retired at the age of sixty-five, and in a recent telephone interview with the author said that he thoroughly enjoyed his time at the London Jewish. It was warm, relaxed and informal, and there were friendly relations between staff and patients. Patients had a sense of personal proprietorship in the Hospital because they had been so closely involved in its establishment. This led to an egalitarian atmosphere; at King's everyone stood to one side as the consultants walked down the corridor, not so at the London Jewish Hospital.

According to an obituary in *Munk's Roll*,[6] Hugh Gainsborough [1893–1980] was in some ways an unlikely person to be on the staff of a West End hospital in the 1930s. He was unmistakably Semitic, and had no time for the affectations sometimes thought necessary for successful private practice. He was educated at Downing College, Cambridge where he was a foundation scholar, and St George's Hospital. At the latter, and at the London Jewish Hospital, he established special diabetic clinics and was one of the first physicians to use insulin in treatment. He was appointed to the St George's staff in 1927 as assistant physician by which time he had already been associated with the London Jewish Hospital for some years. During World War II, he was senior physician and one of the senior members of staff remaining at St George's at Hyde Park Corner. He was a strong advocate of the view that the hospital should be rebuilt at Tooting and not on the same site as had been originally proposed. He took a prominent part until well into the 1960s in the efforts to save the London Jewish Hospital from closure. A keen supporter of the underdog, he would give instinctive support to those he thought likely to be discriminated against because of their race, creed or sex. Some nurses found him a little superior in his attitude to them, but he was generally accepted as a kind and compassionate man.

Edward Gustave Slesinger [1888–1975] was a steadfast Guy's man working for its medical school and hospital for nearly sixty years. The only break in his period of service was during World War I when he served as a Surgeon-Lieutenant in the Royal Navy, being mentioned in despatches and awarded the Croix de Guerre with palm. He was born in London and entered Guy's in 1905. He rose through the ranks there, becoming full surgeon in 1933. He was a consultant surgeon at the London Jewish Hospital both before and after World War II.

Simon Isaac Levy [1899–1959] was born in Liverpool, brought up in Merthyr, and qualified from Westminster Hospital in 1922. He was strictly orthodox. After a short time in general practice, he gained his surgical experience at the Westminster, Guy's, and the Prince of Wales hospitals, and his appointment as surgical registrar at the London Jewish Hospital was one of his first. He also attended at the Bearsted Memorial Hospital. A tall, handsome, dignified man, he had a keen intellect and a lively interest in charitable causes. He served on the Jewish Board of Deputies and was a keen supporter of the Hebrew University in Jerusalem. According to one matron, he was an excellent surgeon, but staff were frightened of him, and silence reigned when he was at work. He could be bad tempered, and was known occasionally to throw instruments. Though he did not speak Yiddish, he understood it very well.

Louis Forman [1901–1988] was at the London Jewish Hospital for more than twenty years from the mid-1920s. He was born at Portsmouth, the eldest son of Itzhak and Annie Sarah Fogelman. Though he was brought up in an orthodox family he was an agnostic, but proudly Jewish. As a student at Guy's he was a gold medal and scholarship winner, and after graduation had an excellent training there as assistant house surgeon and house physician. He fell out with Sir Arthur Hurst, a pioneer in clinical science and a senior physician at Guy's, accusing him of tampering with experimental results. Unsurprisingly, he was not immediately appointed to a medical post there. Medicine's loss was dermatology's gain. He subsequently became consultant physician at Guy's in diseases of the skin, a position he held until 1967. He was also president of the British Association of Dermatology. Colleagues described him as brilliant.

A small man, with thick glasses, he examined every patient minutely, even when others had given up. An excellent teacher, he had a remarkably retentive memory coupled with an encyclopaedic knowledge of his subject that he kept up-to-date even after his retirement. In his last few years a devoted friend read to him for three or four hours daily so that he could maintain his mastery of his chosen subject. Of great charm and good humour, he always thought the best of everyone. He was also a frugal man, going everywhere by bus and tube, and rarely spending money on himself other than on books and his extensive glass collection.

Geoffrey Lawrence Konstam [1899–1962] was the son of a leather tanner and merchant. He was born in London, and went to Heath Mount School at Hampstead and then to Westminster School. His training at King's College Hospital Medical School was interrupted by service in the forces in 1918–1919 as a signals officer in the Far East. After qualifying he was house surgeon and resident anaesthetist at King's College Hospital, and house surgeon in the genito-urinary department there; house physician at the Hampstead General and Paddington Green Children's Hospitals; medical first assistant registrar at the London Hospital; and then medical registrar at the West London Hospital where he obtained a staff appointment in 1931. In 1929 he was appointed assistant physician to the London Jewish Hospital and also held the position of physician at East Ham Memorial Hospital. Never ruffled or hurried, he was an able teacher. From 1940–45 he served in the R.A.M.C. as a lieutenant-colonel in charge of the medical division of the 43rd and 63rd military hospitals. He had a wide circle of friends interested, as he was, in the arts, and in 1961 he retired, giving up a large consulting practice to devote himself to sculpture at which he was a proficient practitioner.

Muriel Elsie Landau [1895–1972] was born in London and educated at Dame Alice Owens School, Islington, where she gained an entrance scholarship to the London School of Medicine for Women. She qualified in 1918, and after house appointments at the Royal Free and at Queen Charlotte's Hospitals was appointed registrar to the Hospital for Women, Soho Square. In 1921, she took her MD in obstetrics and gynaecology, and at the early age of twenty-six was appointed to the staff of the Elizabeth Garrett Anderson Hospital. There she practised general surgery and eventually became senior consulting surgeon, serving the hospital from 1921–1961, the year of her retirement. She was also on the staff of the London Jewish Hospital and the Marie Curie Hospital for women. An outstanding personality, likeable and kind, she acquired a large private practice over a period of some forty-five years. For the years 1965–6 she was President of the Medical Women's Federation of Great Britain.

An ardent Zionist, she was chairman of the Doctors' and Dentists' Group for the Joint Palestine Appeal for more than fifteen years. Her husband, Sammy Sacks, was a well-known and much loved general practitioner in New Road in the East End and later at Mapesbury Road, Brondesbury Park. They had four sons, three of whom became doctors. Their children were playmates of Emmanuel Miller's children. Each family produced an internationally renowned child; Dr Jonathan Miller, the theatrical producer and man of many parts, and Oliver Sacks, the author of several best-selling books on psychiatry.

Emmanuel Miller [1893–1970] was the youngest of the nine children of orthodox Lithuanian parents who had emigrated to England. His father was known as a 'healer' in the *shtetl* in which he lived, but became a furrier after he arrived in London. Emmanuel was born in the family house in Fournier Street, Spitalfields that doubled as a workshop, and Emmanuel, along with the other children in the family, was lulled to sleep by the whirr of sewing machines. He attended Jews' Free School, Parmiter's School, and the City of London School, and was awarded an exhibition at St John's College, Cambridge. From there he went to the London Hospital, eventually being elected F.R.C.P. Probably his most important post was that of physician to the Maudsley Hospital.

From his early twenties he referred to himself as a medical psychologist, and in 1927 founded the East London Child Guidance Clinic, the first properly constituted institution of its kind in Britain. It was originally housed in rooms at the Jews' Free School, but during World War II moved to the London Jewish Hospital where it remained for many years as an important adjunct to the Hospital.

A fine looking man and an excellent teacher, his students held him in great affection, and deeply appreciated his warm understanding of their problems. He wrote widely on child psychiatry and child guidance. He was fluent in Hebrew, though not Yiddish, and sculpted, drew, etched and painted with great talent.

Samuel Barnet Dimson [1907–1991] was born in London, the son of Zacharia Dimson, a minister of religion. From the Davenant Foundation School, Sam Dimson went on to University College Hospital and combined it with a course at Jews' College where he was trained as a rabbi. He decided not to pursue the family tradition and concentrated instead on medicine. His talmudic training and family background were possibly responsible for his love of teaching at which he excelled.

After qualifying he held house posts at Sheffield Royal Infirmary and Queen Mary's Hospital, London. From 1934–36 he was clinical assistant at the Queen Elizabeth Hospital for Children, London, where he acquired his interest in paediatrics. He enlisted in the R.A.M.C. in World War II, holding the rank of major and serving in Sierra Leone, India and Burma. During the last three years of the war he held the rank of lieutenant colonel in command of a medical division and was mentioned in despatches. He became a physician in the Children's Department of the London Jewish Hospital after his demobilisation, and was consultant paediatrician to the Sydenham Children's Hospital, Queen Mary's Hospital for the East End, and East Ham Memorial Hospital. He was the first to introduce unlimited visiting in the children's ward. 'Very nice and gentle, he treated all his patients with tender loving care'. He also carried on a private practice at 87 Harley Street, and contributed many articles to medical journals on his specialised subject.

Quiet, and rather shy, he could nonetheless be assertive and forceful, particularly when the welfare of children was in question. At the London Jewish Hospital he actively encouraged children of all ethnic groups to attend his department and this was a particularly noticeable feature of the Hospital in the years before its closure. His attitude to life and to his work was illustrated when he broke his ankle in a skiing accident. Instead of making it an excuse to take sick leave, he appeared at his clinic on crutches and declared his good fortune in having broken his left ankle and not his right, so still being able to drive his car that had automatic transmission.

Hannah Hedwig Striesow (nee Kohn), who was born in Bamberg in Germany in 1908, also has an unusual background. She began training as a doctor at the Medical Faculty of the University of Halle, Germany in 1927, passing the final examination in December 1932. She then went to the Barmbecker Hospital in Hamburg in January 1933 for her probationary year, but in April all its Jewish doctors and consultants were dismissed except for its two probationers, who were kept on till they finished their year. She left in January 1934, and in 1936, unable to practise as a doctor in England without the necessary English qualifications, she became a probationer nurse at the London Jewish Hospital, qualifying as a state registered nurse in December 1939. She married in that month, and according to the then regulations should have resigned from her post, but only the matron and Mr Pitt, the Secretary, knew of her marriage, and they kept it to themselves. She worked as a staff nurse until May 1940 when Holland fell to the Germans and all the German refugee staff were dismissed (though reinstated some months later). She returned in January 1947, having worked at other hospitals in the interim, and became the out-patient sister.

In 1948, Parliament passed a law that aliens with overseas qualifications as doctors who had rendered valuable war service in the United Kingdom should be permitted to practise without taking further examinations. She fell into this category. Her application for registration was supported by Gordon, Prieskel, David Levi, S. I. Levy and Konstam, and in 1950 she was admitted to the Medical Register and transformed, overnight, from sister to house surgeon.

She successfully applied to acquire a general practitioner's practice in Forest Gate, but was short of £2,000 to complete the purchase. When her colleagues learned of this, they arranged a loan for her. David Levi, Israel Prieskel, Albert Davis, Elsie Landau, Anthony Radcliffe, Geoffrey Konstam, S. I. Levy and J. Rabinowitch the radiologist, made loans totalling £1,700, and Sam Dimson acted as guarantor at her bank for £300. She repaid them all within five years. No one asked for interest. She continued in general practice for forty years, specialising in obstetrics and acting as a Police Surgeon for practically the whole period.

David Levi joined the Hospital in 1945, and was one of the most brilliant of its consultants. Short, and rather brusque, he was 'the busiest surgeon in town and possibly the best'. His reputation was of the highest. Quick and efficient, he was in every way a superior surgeon. It was said of him that 'later in his career, when he was a frail old man, he became young when a scalpel was in his hands'.

Harold Avery, a physician at the Hospital during the 1930s had an East End background. Leopold Mandel, the physician, appointed in 1915 and still on the active staff in 1947, was one of the Lyons catering family. David Krestin, an honorary physician from 1919 until nationalisation, was described by the nursing staff as 'an absolute darling'. He also practised at University College Hospital and at Charing Cross Hospital.

Anthony Radcliffe, F.R.C.S., D.L.O., and a Fellow of the Royal Society of Medicine, was born in Cape Town in 1907 and was educated at Cape Town University and Trinity College, Dublin. He qualified in 1930, and after some time at Hemel Hamstead Hospital obtained the position of house surgeon at West London Hospital, a post-graduate hospital. He spent a month at the London Hospital in 1937 on a course, and felt that the Jewish patients there were patronised, and not equally treated. He joined the London Jewish Hospital in 1938, and shortly afterwards took up his position at the Royal National Ear Nose and Throat Hospital at Golden Square. He served in the Royal Air Force 1940–6. In response to the question put to him by the author, 'Why have a Jewish hospital?' his reply was 'Why not?'

Two of the porters were a Mr Cohen and a Mr Solomon.

WORLD WAR II – 1939–45

Prior to the outbreak of World War II it could generally be said that the London Jewish was a first class hospital carrying out excellent work for its patients, but there were criticisms from a minority of the members of the Hospital's Medical Committee. These came to a head when a memorandum of 21 June 1938 was submitted to the Chairman of the Hospital, Major F. M. Green, by Arnold Sorsby, Harold Avery, Maurice Sorsby, A. D. Woolf and R. Hamburger.[1] They felt there was a downward trend in the Hospital's efficiency and prestige. There had been several resignations from the surgical department in the previous two years, and the fact that there was no waiting list for surgery was interpreted not as a sign of efficiency, rather that the poor were not being attracted to the hospital. They complained that the medical department dealt with a higher proportion of cases of those over fifty years of age compared with other local voluntary hospitals, and it was being looked upon as a Home for Aged Jews. They further said that the consultant in-patient physician visited the wards only once a week, compared with twice at similar hospitals. 'In practice this means the patients are under the supervision of the house physician, who, though the senior of the residents is practically always a relatively inexperienced man, and one whose opinion the local practitioners do not consider to be as good as their own. This inevitably leads to a lack of confidence in the hospital'.

The writers felt their previous suggestions had been sidetracked, and that the Medical Committee no longer functioned as a dispassionate advisory body. They called for a drastic re-organisation of the work of both the medical and the surgical departments and pinpointed Julius Burnford as the main culprit for holding up necessary reforms. However, nothing was resolved about these complaints before the War began, and rumblings of discontent continued.

Immediately the war began, an Emergency Medical Service under the control of the Ministry of Health was introduced, giving central government a right of direction over both voluntary and municipal hospitals, a right it had never previously possessed. In contrast to the First World War when the emergency plans were based on the need to provide adequate hospital facilities for wounded soldiers and sailors, those for World War II were dominated by the perceived need to provide hospital care for civilians wounded by air attack. During the early days of the war 140,000 patients in London hospitals were discharged, or evacuated to outlying hospitals, to make room for the expected vast casualties, and many of the staff followed them.

London's hospitals were required to reserve a high percentage of their beds for use by the Ministry, and during 1940 the London Jewish Hospital had fifty beds in use, only twenty of which were allowed for civilian occupation. The pressure on this accommodation was considerable, particularly as many of the medical and surgical staff had been called into the armed services.

Despite the casualties that followed the evacuation from Dunkirk and the London blitz of 1940–1, the Emergency Medical Service was never placed under the stress that had been predicted and for which it had been designed, serious though the damage from bombing proved to be. There was a surplus of available beds for bombing victims by quite a margin, but fear of a possible increase kept beds empty.

One effect of the emergency was that doctors and nurses for the first time moved freely between the voluntary and the municipal hospitals, seeing the problems each faced. Even during the early stages of the war, consideration was being given by Churchill's government to its post-war hospital policy. From January to September 1941, a Ministry committee was at work and had a preliminary paper laid before it containing proposals remarkably similar to those that ultimately formed the basis of the National Health Service Act of 1946. In October, the government announced that after the war it would propose a single service organised by the local authorities, in which the voluntary and municipal hospitals would co-operate. A hospital survey for London was instituted to provide a firm basis for planning.

A joint co-ordinating committee established by the King's Fund and the Voluntary Hospitals Committee issued its own report. It viewed freedom of choice for the patient as essential, and opposed the government's idea of a single system, believing that standards were maintained by competition, and that the voluntary hospitals provided the standard by which public hospitals could be judged. Implementation of any scheme had, of necessity, to be postponed until after the war's end, and hospitals had no option but to carry on under the existing system, and on the assumption that their basic position would remain unchanged.

An article in the London *Evening Standard* of 7 May 1942, ominously headlined 'London's Little Hospitals Doomed', carried a prophetic warning for smaller hospitals such as the London Jewish Hospital:

The majority of the capital's smaller establishments will disappear after the war. That is the view of the medical experts representing both municipal and voluntary hospitals, appointed by the Ministry of Health ... the smaller unit is not nearly so suited to modern hospital treatment as the big establishment, both economically and administratively.

Few London hospitals escaped bomb damage. The London Jewish Hospital was hit on the night of Tuesday, 15 October 1940. There is an undated report on the bombing signed by Dr Burnford, then resident Medical Superintendent of the Hospital, and M Hampshire, the Matron:[2]

Tuesday, 15 October 1940
At 11.8 p.m. a bomb exploded on the low office building adjoining the Hospital in the confined space between the Hospital and the Synagogue building.[3] The office building caught fire immediately and the gas pipes outside the Hospital broke and blazed up. All the wards were devastated, windows blown in, and the partition walls destroyed and debris piled up.

The first floor wards were housing the patients under the care of a sister and five nurses: Sister Wood and nurses Neukorn, Berkman, Frolich, Turtledove and Cross. The behaviour of these sister and nurses deserve special mention. Owing in great part to their coolness and calm demeanour the patients were removed from the wards, in the dark, and transferred to waiting ambulances. Sister Wood in particular directed her staff with conspicuous skill and did not rest until all her nurses had been accounted for. Unfortunately Nurse Berkman and Nurse Frolich were badly injured and had to be removed at the outset to the London Hospital.

The Resident Medical Officer, though injured also, aided manfully before going to the London Hospital for treatment. Mr Brodie, Assistant Secretary, was severely traumatised. Notwithstanding this, and the fact that a few days previously he had been blown up on a bus in the street, he was a pillar of strength. Owing to his initiative the gas was turned off, and the blaze extinguished. When all was quiet, and only then, he was persuaded to go to the London Hospital where he was detained for treatment. Of the porters, several were injured, but two of the remainder, porter Kemp and carpenter Overett, quickly went to the roof, kitchen, and stores and spent over an hour in quenching several fires which had broken out in the stores and escaped the notice of the firemen. Matron would like to stress the good work of Sister Wood and the three nurses who were uninjured, namely Nurses Cross, Neukorn, and Turtledove.

As a result of this we are pleased to say that no patient suffered further injury. One patient in particular who had just been admitted with a perforated duodenal ulcer was being prepared for an operation and he was transferred and successfully operated upon in Mile End Hospital immediately.

For ourselves, we are proud to be associated with so fine a team of workers.

The offices, boardroom and the old Nurses' Home were destroyed, and the main building was devastated by the blast. The new Nurses' Home was undamaged.

It was obvious that large sections of the Hospital would remain unusable for a long time; as a temporary measure the ground floor of the Nurses' Home was adapted as a hospital unit with an operating theatre and small wards It was not until April 1941, on the eve of Passover, that the patched-up wards were brought back into service with a complement of seventy beds, forty of which were reserved for casualties. Throughout, the Hospital continued treating every in-patient or out-patient in need of urgent attention, and for this great credit was due not only to the efforts of the medical staff but also of its secretary, Mr George Pitt.

Almost all the Hospital's records were destroyed by the bombing, and strenuous efforts were made to reconstitute the list of governors and other donors. An appeal was made in the Annual Report for 1940 for continued assistance:

> Increasing difficulties of present conditions and rising prices make it imperative that the support hitherto received shall not diminish if the Hospital is to continue its ministrations to all who have need of its help and assistance. We would emphasise that, apart from the contributions received from the Ministry of Health for the maintenance of the beds reserved for war casualties, the amount received from other sources, including the awards of the King Edward's Hospital Fund and Hospital Sunday Fund, provided only 52% of the Maintenance expenditure ... It is therefore essential that the pre-war volume of voluntary gifts shall be maintained if the Hospital is to continue its work and finally to take its part in post-war reconstruction, not only as a Hospital, but as a centre of cultural life for the Jewish Medical profession.

The staff was boosted by the appointment of two doctors, presumably refugees from Hitler, who had only foreign qualifications but who were placed upon the Temporary Medical Register of the General Medical Council. The Ladies' Aid Association continued its useful work.

In 1942, the Ophthalmic out-patient department under Dr Pines was re-opened, and during 1943 other out-patient clinics operated as normally as possible; total attendances were 21,000 compared with 80,000 pre-war. Arrangements were put in hand to re-open the children's ward. There were, on average, twenty-three nurses at the Hospital during the year, seven trained and sixteen (all but three Jewish) student nurses. Many of the Jewish nurses had come to England as refugees and played a prominent part in maintaining services and standards.

Voluntary gifts increased from £5,181 to £6,025, and the governors reiterated their intention to restore the Hospital to its former glory after the war. They said they were convinced that a Jewish hospital had to be in the forefront of progress. That would cost money, but they expressed their confidence that the vital greater support from the community would be forthcoming.[4]

Arnold Sorsby gave up his office of Honorary Ophthalmic Surgeon in 1943 on his appointment as the first holder of the Research Chair in Ophthalmology at the Royal College of Surgeons. Whether his new position left him no time, or whether he used it as an excuse to leave an institution with which he was to some extent discontented, is not clear.

Towards the end of 1945, Dr David Krestin, Dr Geoffrey Konstam, and Mr Anthony Radcliffe returned from war service, and the Child Guidance Clinic reopened. The work of reparation of war damage started, but was hampered by the need to obtain building permission and, most importantly, by the national shortage of materials and labour.

Hugh Gainsborough returned to duty on his release from the Emergency Medical Service. Julius Burnford and Harold Kisch retired from the active staff in accordance with the Hospital's regulations, but continued as Consulting Staff. They were the last two of the original members of the Honorary Medical Staff, and had served as Medical Officers and taken part in the administrative work, both on the Council and on the Medical Committee. Burnford had been Chairman of the latter for upwards of twenty-five years, and had rendered particularly invaluable service during the war years.

Lord Rothschild was President. Bernhard Baron's son, Sir Edward Baron was Treasurer to the Building Fund. The Honorary Presidents were James de Rothschild and Goodman Levy, and Lady Sassoon was the Honorary Vice-President. J. Cofman Nicoresti who with his wife had rendered twenty-five years service to the Hospital, was on the Council of Management.

THE HOSPITAL OPENS

[1] A copy of the speech is in the Gaster papers.

[2] The divisions and jealousies aroused by the movement still ran high. Goodman Levy invited his friend Sir Edwin Cooper Perry, the Superintendent of Guy's, founder of the Royal Army Medical College, and a former consultant at the London Hospital, to the opening. He declined, saying he feared Viscount Knutsford would 'take it as a somewhat unfriendly act if I should publicly associate myself with a new Hospital popularly, though I hope erroneously, regarded as a rival claimant for the support of the Hebrew Community'. Southampton Archives MS 116/45.

[3] *Jewish Chronicle*, 31 October 1919.

[4] Sir Alfred Mond, the founder of I.C.I. had been invited to perform the opening ceremony, but was unable to attend.

[5] Subscribers were requested, before they granted letters of recommendation, to ascertain so far as possible that applicants were not persons who could afford to pay for medical assistance.

[6] At this time, the cost of each out-patient visit was calculated to be 2/11d.

[7] In 1921 there were ten branch committees. Five were in the East End, two in West London, and one each in the City, South London, and North-West London. In 1926 there were just six branches, only one of which was in the East End.

[8] The author is indebted to Berliner's grandson, the late Mr Cyril Lewis, for this information.

[9] 18 December 1925.

[10] 24 December 1925.

[11] Goodman Levy was twice offered the position, but declined because he thought it would be in the best interests of the Hospital for someone with a higher public profile, and an influential position within and without the community, to be appointed. He was later appointed an Honorary President.

[12] Between 1929 and 1949 the trustees of his Charitable funds gave a further £24,480.

[13] *Jewish Chronicle*, 15 October 1926.

THE HOSPITAL IN THE 1920s AND 1930s

[1] The author has drawn heavily in this section on a history of the Society to 1964 set out in the Presidential Address of Dr Laurence Phillips delivered on 22 October 1964.

[2] Until 1936, meetings were held at the Hospital, but the Society then used more central locations including B.M.A. House and Woburn House. After the war the Medical Society of London offered facilities at its premises in Chandos Place, and that is where many of its meetings are held today. The presidential badge bears the inscription from Ben Sira, 'The skill of the physician exalteth him'.

[3] Julius Burnford; E. C. Hughes; A. H. Levy; H. A. Kisch; D. N. Nabarro; L. Mandel; J. Lauer; H. Gainsborough; S. I. Levy; E. G. Slesinger; D. Krestin; G. Konstam; H. S. Souttar; Elsie Landau; L. Forman; A. A. Davis; I. Prieskel; I. Gordon; S. B. Dimson; A. Radcliffe; E. Miller; and Dr Striesow.

[4] In an interview with Jenny Abrahams in 1982. The section on Dr Pines is largely based on that interview.

[5] Presidential Address delivered by Dr L. Phillips on 22 October 1964 to the London Jewish Medical Society.

[6] Volume vii, p. 197.

WORLD WAR II – 1939–45

[1] At London Metropolitan Archives. Ref: A/KE/244.

[2] At London Metropolitan Archives. Ref: A/KE/244.

[3] This refers to the East London Synagogue next door to the Hospital.

[4] Because of the reduced civilian use of the Hospital, and payments from the Ministry of Health for caring for casualties, income exceeded expenditure between 1939–45, strengthening the Hospital's balance sheet.

6

LIST OF BRANCHES
and their gross Returns for 1919.

EAST LONDON BRANCH No. 1.
Chairman : J. L. Berman.
Vice-Chairman : S. Leverick.
Treasurer : M. Landau.
Hon. Secretary : Miss L. Kozlovsky, 128, Mile End Road, E. 1.
Gross Receipts £1,185 11 3½

EAST LONDON BRANCH No. 2.
Chairman : J. Starr.
Vice-Chairman : J. Jacobs.
Treasurer : J. Gutchman.
Secretary : D. Harris, 26, Newnham Street, E. 1.
Gross Receipts £352 15 10

EAST LONDON BRANCH No. 3.
Chairman : M. Lipman.
Vice-Chairmen : S. Rabinovitch and A. Goldman.
Treasurer : S. Wolkind.
Hon. Secretary : M. Harris, 67, Jubilee Street, E. 1.
Gross Receipts £294 9 6

CITY BRANCH No. 4.
Chairman : A. Alexander.
Vice-Chairmen : P. Yanover and Mrs. I. R. Kornblum.
Treasurer : C. Abrahams.
Hon. Secretary : H. Greenstein, 37, Spital Square, E.C. 1.
Gross Receipts £489 4 5

SOUTH LONDON BRANCH No. 5.
Chairman : N. White.
Vice-Chairman : K. Merron.
Treasurer : E. Ring.
Hon. Secretary : M. Gabriel, Flat 2, 23, St. Anne's Road, Brixton, S.W. 2.

Forward ... £2,322 1 0½

7

Forward ... £2,322 1 0½

NORTH LONDON BRANCH
Gross Receipts £170 12 0

WEST LONDON BRANCH No. 7.
Chairman : Dr. A. Goodman Levy.
Vice-Chairman : B. Bull.
Treasurer : Mrs. A. G. Levy.
Hon. Secretary: Mr. Staby, 21, Markham Square, Chelsea, S.W. 3.
Gross Receipts £341 11 7½

NORTH-WEST LONDON BRANCH No. 8.
President: Mrs. Friedlander.
Chairman : M. Michaelis.
Treasurer : Mrs. H. Wolff.
Hon. Secretary : Mrs. J. Cofman-Nicoresti, 16, Crediton Hill, N.W. 3.
Gross Receipts £1,930 7 4

EAST LONDON BRANCH No. 9.
Chairman : Mrs. A. Straker.
Vice-Chairmen : Mrs. B. Botzman, Mrs. Davis and Mrs. Deitch.
Treasurer : Mrs. J. Kipernick.
Hon. Secretary : J. B. Swager, 8, John's Place, Clark Street, E. 1.
Gross Receipts £325 2 1

EAST LONDON BRANCH No. 12.
Chairman : O. Sapolinsky.
Vice-Chairman : S. Levitt.
Treasurer : B. Nathan.
Hon. Secretary : H. Ostrick, 23, Boreham Street, E. 1.
Gross Receipts £77 9 11½

Total £5,167 4 0½

Funds remitted direct to Head Office ... £5,153 10 7½

Gross Amount as per Income and Expenditure Account ... £10,320 14 8

List of branches in 1919.

(XXIII)

(XXIV) *The London Hospital outpatient waiting room. Waiting time could be up to seven hours.*
[*London Hospital Archives*]

(XXV)   *London Jewish Hospital out-patient department waiting room.*

1919.

צדקה ומרפא.

Fifth Annual Report

OF THE

London Jewish Hospital,

STEPNEY GREEN, E. 1.

GEO. BARBER, Printer, The Furnival Press, Furnival Street, E.C.4.

(XXVI)   *Front page of 1919 Annual Report.*

Commemorations.

Permanent help may be given to the Hospital by means of a donation to commemorate a name either in perpetuity or during the lifetime of the donor.

The Committee, believing that no more appropriate way could be found, venture to recommend this means of perpetuating the memory of deceased relatives and friends.

This may be done in consideration of donations as follows:—

	Ward. £	Bed. £	Cot. £
In Perpetuity	5000	1000	500
During Life of Donor	—	500	250
Annually, by Subscription	—	50	30

MEMORIAL TABLETS will be placed in the **Waiting Hall** of the Hospital on payment of the following **Donations**:—

Size, 12 inches × 6 inches   ..   ..   ..   **50 guineas.**

,, 14 inches × 10 inches   ..   ..   ..   **100 guineas.**

Donations of £25 and upwards will be inscribed on a Roll in the Entrance Hall of the Hospital.

Small Rooms may be named on payment of a sum to be approved by the Council of Management.

(XXVII) *Commemorations by naming cots, beds and wards were an important source of income.*

צדקה ומרפא

LONDON JEWISH HOSPITAL

FOUNDED 1907

THIS IS TO CERTIFY THAT

V. Berliner Esq.

WAS ELECTED A LIFE GOVERNOR

IN CONSIDERATION OF *his* BENEFACTIONS

TO THIS INSTITUTION.

I. Berliner — President

W. Tephany — Secretary

30th August 1920

(XXVIII) *Life Governor's certificate issued to Isador Berliner's son, Victor. He served the Hospital for thirty years.* *[Mrs Enid Rosenberg]*

Jewish World
December 8, 1921.

THE JEW AND PEACE.

[REG.G.P.O. AS A NEWSPAPER.]

ESTABLISHED 1873.

THE JEWISH WORLD

AN ANGLO-JEWISH JOURNAL

FOR EVERYJEW

[No. 2,543.   Thursday, December 8, 1921—Kislev 7, 5682.   Two Pence

ONE OF THE WARDS

THE FRONTAGE

ANOTHER OF THE WARDS

THE OPERATING THEATRE

DR. A. GOODMAN LEVY.
COUNCIL CHAIRMAN.

MR. S. LEVERICK.
EAST LONDON BRANCH.

MR. HENRY WOLFF.
VICE PRESIDENT.

MRS. B. FRIEDLANDER.
VICE PRESIDENT.

THE CHIEF RABBI.
HON. PRESIDENT.

MR. G. E. PITT.
SECRETARY.

MR. J. BERLINER.
PRESIDENT.

MRS. NEWMAN.
MATRON.

LORD ROTHSCHILD.
HONORARY PRESIDENT.

HAHAM GASTER.
HON. PRESIDENT.

MR. E. B. KAPP.
VICE PRESIDENT.

DR. A. GASTER.
HON. TREASURER.

MR. ALBERT M. COHN.
VICE PRESIDENT.

MR. L. LIEBSTER.
VICE PRESIDENT.

The Chief Rabbi, Lord Rothschild and others at the opening ceremony last Sunday.

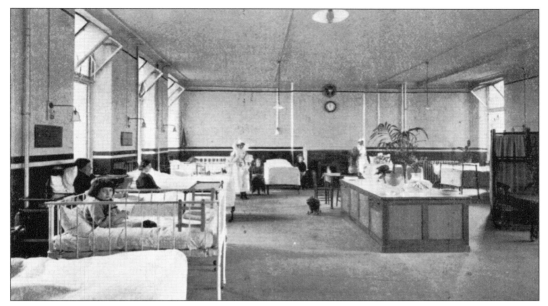

(XXXI) *Female medical ward in 1921.*

27

Beds Named.

Beds and Cots may be named in consideration of the following donations :—

	Ward. £	Bed. £	Cot. £
In Perpetuity	5000 ...	1000 ...	500
During Life of Donor	— ...	500 ...	250
Annually, by Subscription	— ...	50 ...	30

DATE.	NAME OF BED.	WARD.
1919	The Ramah Ezra ...	Medical, Female
1920	The Branch No. 1 ...	,, ,,
1920	The Elias Meyer ...	Koenigsberg
1921	The Richard Phillips ...	Medical, Female
1921	The Daniel de Pass ...	Koenigsberg
1921	The Louis Adler... ...	,,
1921	The Simon Festenstein	,,
1921	The Fanny Festenstein	Medical, Female
1921	The Marian Levy ...	,, ,,
1922	The Abraham & Millie Gold & Maurie Gold Bed	,, ,,

(XXXII)   *Beds named between 1919 and 1921.*

(XXXIII) *Isidor Berliner and his son Victor on holiday in Wiesbaden in the 1920s.*

[*Mrs Enid Rosenberg*]

(XXXIV) *Berliner's memorial stone at Marlow Road Cemetery.*

[*Mrs Anita Black*]

LONDON JEWISH HOSPITAL FLAG DAY : LITERARY SOCIETIES' GARDEN PARTY : A FETE.

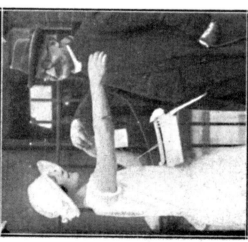

LONDON JEWISH HOSPITAL FLAG DAY.—The annual Flag Day of the London Jewish Hospital held last Sunday was again a great success. On the left is a snapshot of the "Jewish Bishop of Stepney" buying a flag. In the centre is a group of helpers, including (on right) the local "Pearly King." On the right is a portrait of Mr. B. V. Spivack, the Assistant Secretary of the Hospital, who, together with Mr. G. E. Pitt, the Secretary, was responsible for the arrangements.

[JEWISH WORLD Photos.]

(XXXV)　　*Flag Day, June 1925. The 'Jewish Bishop of Stepney' was Rev. J. F. Stern, the minister at East London Synagogue.*

[Mrs Edith Spivack]

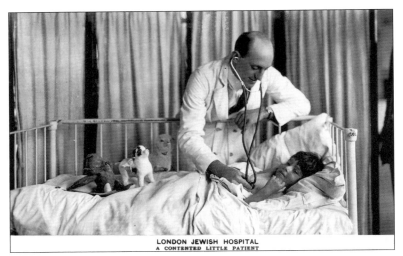

(XXXVI)

(XXXVII)

Postcards sent to prospective donors. No opportunity was missed to raise funds.

צדקה ומרפא

LONDON JEWISH HOSPITAL
STEPNEY GREEN, E. 1.

The sick and ailing patients of the London
Jewish Hospital send you their congratulations and
best wishes on the birth of your son.
    Will you commemorate the happy event by sending
a donation or subscription to the funds of the
Hospital ?

Hon. President.

Message on back of the postcards.

(XXXVIII) *Staff photograph in 1920s.*

[Mr Brian Gordon]

(XXXIX)

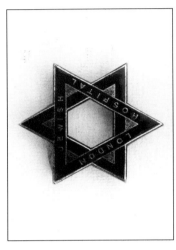

(XL)   *Nurse's belt and badge.*
[*Mrs Joy Lyons*]

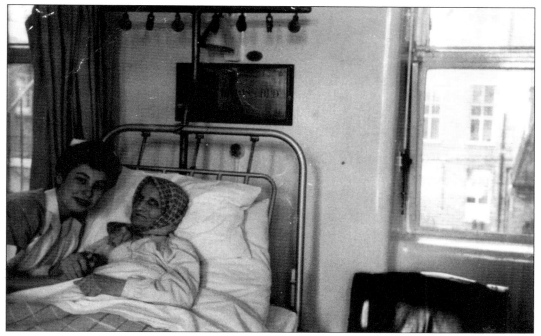

(XLI) *Ninety year old patient in 1960s. She spoke only Yiddish. The nurse is Suzanne Leigh.*

[*Mrs Suzanne Leigh*]

(XLII) *Children's ward in the 1960s.* [*Mr Brian Gordon*]

(XLIII) *Prize giving day 1960. In the back row are Mr Bullock, the nursing tutor, Gloria Spurling, Margaret Dixon, Suzanne Leigh (then Haziza), third from right, and Miriam Joseph. In the front row, the Matron, Mr A. Radcliffe, Mrs Ewan Montagu, Mr J. Samuel, Her Worship the Mayor of Stepney, councillor Mrs A. Elboz, and at end of row Mr Jack Magrill, the Hospital secretary.*

[Mrs Suzanne Leigh]

LONDON JEWISH HOSPITAL,
STEPNEY GREEN, E.1.

LETTER OF RECOMMENDATION.

I RECOMMEND _____ as a Patient of the LONDON JEWISH HOSPITAL

_____ aged _____

Occupation _____

Address _____

Subscriber's Signature _____

Address _____

Date _____ 192___

Before granting Letters of Recommendation, Subscribers are requested to ascertain, as far as possible, that applicants are not persons whose position and means enable them to pay for medical assistance, but such persons may be admitted for consultation, if they bring a letter from their Doctor recommending them to the Visiting Physician for consultation.

OUT-PATIENT DEPARTMENT.

The Patient must bring this letter to the Out-Patient Department at the times stated overleaf. This letter entitles the patient to treatment for a period of three months.

__Accidents and urgent cases are seen at all times without a letter.__

IN-PATIENT DEPARTMENT.

If In-patient treatment is deemed necessary by a Member of the Medical and Surgical Staff no further letter will be required, and cases so recommended will be notified as soon as accommodation can be found for them.

Patients holding a Letter seeking admission as In-patients must attend the Out-patient Department, on any day (excepting Saturday and Sunday) at one o'clock, for examination by a Member of the Out-patient Staff. Accidents and urgent cases are admitted at all times without a letter provided accommodation is available.

Patients residing at a distance from the Hospital may apply for admission by forwarding this letter by post, together with a letter from the Patient's doctor. Such patients should not attend the Hospital until requested to do so.

The following are unsuitable for admission as In-patients:—

(a) Persons who, upon examination, are found to be suffering from incurable diseases.

(b) Persons suffering from chronic complaints, which are so tedious of cure as to preclude the admission of more urgent cases.

(c) Cases requiring merely rest.

(d) Cases of mental diseases.

(e) Patients who in the opinion of the Hospital authorities, would be more suitably treated at a Poor Law Institution.

(f) Those capable of receiving adequate treatment as Out-patients.

(g) Those suffering from infective fevers, and acute Venereal disease.

All patients accepted for In-patient treatment should be prepared to answer questions regarding their circumstances. They will be required to contribute towards the cost of maintenance, according to their means.

In-patients are expected to be furnished with a change of linen, a towel, and soap, knife, fork, and spoon, and a brush, and comb.

They are also expected to provide for their own washing, and to provide their tea, butter, and sugar.

Patients are forbidden to receive any other provisions from their friends, except eggs. In-patients having money or other valuables must give them into the care of the Sister of the ward: otherwise the Hospital cannot be responsible for their safety.

VISITING DAYS.

Wednesdays	-	3 - 4 o'clock.
Saturday	-	3 - 4.30 o'clock.

TIMES OF ATTENDANCE FOR OUT-PATIENTS.

MEDICAL CASES	Daily at 1 p.m. except Saturday and Sunday.
SURGICAL CASES	Friday at 9 a.m.
DISEASES OF WOMEN	Friday at 1 p.m.
DISEASES OF THE EYE	Tuesday at 8.30 a.m.
DISEASES OF THE EAR, NOSE & THROAT	Thursday at 8.30 a.m.
DISEASES OF THE SKIN	Thursday at 1 p.m.

(XLIV) *Except in cases of emergency, in the 1920s prospective patients needed a letter of recommendation before they could be admitted.*

(XLV) *The London Independent Hospital was built on the site of the London Jewish Hospital. Present at an open day were Suzanne Leigh, Dr H. Striesow, Dr Ian Gordon, Maja Jacobs, and Naomi Roland.*

[Mrs Suzanne Leigh]

The London
Jewish Hospital
After Nationalisation

THE INTRODUCTION OF
THE NATIONAL HEALTH SERVICE

After the infirmaries were converted into municipal hospitals by the Local Government Act of 1929, and were taken over by the county and borough authorities, they underwent considerable improvement. The very existence of the voluntary hospital system was once again called into question. The seriousness of the situation led the British Hospital Association to establish a commission, chaired by Lord Sankey, to examine the administration, management and finance of the voluntary hospitals. The report, published in 1937, stated that future prospects were not favourable, and recommended major changes, all involving some loss of control.

The Labour Party's election victory in 1945 radically altered the outlook. The new government believed the state should guarantee a health service free to all at the point of delivery. The voluntary hospitals wanted to keep their independence, but lacked the financial resources to do so. The local authorities were eager to add to their services, but were not prepared to share any of their existing powers with the governors of the voluntary hospitals. The doctors wanted a major say in the direction of the hospital system.

The government's plans provided that the voluntary hospitals would be taken over by the state and run by appointed management committees who would assume the role of the House Committees and Boards of Governors. In vain did the British Hospitals Association argue that it was not in the interests of patients to eliminate all sense of local pride, interest, and responsibility in local hospitals; in vain was it claimed that the trust funds of the voluntary hospitals would be diverted to purposes other than that for which they were intended. Given the government's overwhelming parliamentary majority, the introduction of the National Health Service was inevitable.

It was clear that because patients in National Health hospitals would be entitled to free treatment, hospitals that still charged patients, albeit not the full cost of their treatment, would find demand for their services withering away. Announcements made by the Minister of Health, Aneurin Bevan, had already dried up the large subscriptions. The London Jewish Hospital and almost every other voluntary hospital felt obliged to enter the scheme.

There was considerable debate about the relationship that should exist between the doctors and the state. At one extreme were those who argued that beyond securing the proper education of doctors, and providing a sanitary service to safeguard the drains and control epidemics, the state should leave the medical profession alone to carry out its work in absolute independence of all government control. At the other extreme were those who proposed that all doctors should be state employed, by compulsion if necessary. Partly due to the strong line taken by the medical profession in discussion with Aneurin Bevan, the subsequent Act was far less radical than might have been expected, and differed little from that which a Conservative government would probably have introduced. There was to be no state control of the doctors. Bevan accepted and respected the liberty of the patient to choose his doctor, and the freedom of the doctor to treat his patients according to his own conscience.

The state 'seizure' of their buildings, endowments, and trust funds was hard for the voluntary hospitals to swallow.[1] Bevan planned to redistribute these assets to Regional Boards to reflect 'the actual needs of each rather than the largely accidental effect of past benefactions'. In return for being deprived of their inheritance, the hospitals had the benefit of having all their outstanding debts paid, and were told that in future they would be wholly funded by government out of central taxation, The entire cost of rebuilding, maintaining, and running the hospitals was now to be taken over by the Ministry. There would, it was claimed, be no further need for impassioned appeals to the generosity of the public; private finance providing health services for the poor was to be a thing of the past. Importantly, senior medical consultant staff who had given their services in a strictly honorary capacity were now to be paid in proportion to the time they gave. Bevan said his plan would make Great Britain the envy of the world, and a bright future was promised for its hospitals.

Sectarian hospitals such as the London Jewish Hospital were concerned about their sectarian status, and the London Jewish Hospital had viewed the National Health Service Bill with some misgivings. Bevan addressed these fears in a House of Commons debate on 23 May 1946:

> It must be regarded as a principle of fundamental importance that their special sectarian character must be preserved, because for the people who believe in it, that in itself will be part of the therapy and the treatment. That a Jewish person in a Jewish hospital should be able to continue the rituals of his religion in hospital is an essential part of his treatment ... and that applies to Catholic hospitals. If they are to be brought in, it must be the

obligation of the Regional Boards in establishing the management team to see that these management committees are of the character which maintains the continuity of the characteristics of those institutions. I think I can give that absolute guarantee because otherwise it would be an emotional mutilation that nobody could possibly defend.

Section 61 of the National Health Service Act provided:

Where the character and associations of any voluntary hospital ... are such as link it with a particular religious denomination, regard should be had in the general administration of the hospital and in the making of appointments to the Hospital Management Committee to the preservation and associations of the hospital.

The words, 'regard should be had' were rather more vague than 'an absolute guarantee'.

In its Annual Report for 1947, the Governors took their last opportunity to record their gratitude to all whose generous spirit had given the Hospital support over the previous twenty-nine years:

The London Jewish Hospital has ended its career as a Voluntary Hospital after twenty-nine years of honourable service. It is starting a new life under Nationalisation, but its ideals remain unaltered. It will remain a hospital where sick Jewish men and women can go to be nursed, in an institution that preserves the spirit of Judaism. The founders of the Hospital can be satisfied that their ideals will not be forgotten, and that the London Jewish Hospital will go from strength to strength and will play a worthy part in the new Health Service.
(Signed) F. M. Green, Chairman. G. E. Pitt, Secretary and House Governor

They emphasised that the new regime did not mean that charitable gifts would no longer be acceptable or necessary. Future contributions could he used to provide additional amenities for patients and retain facilities for religious observance.

On 5 July 1948, the London Jewish Hospital's assets were taken over and, in common with all institutions entering the National Health Service, its governing body dissolved. The Council of Management handed over a hospital free of debt.

A new administrative hierarchy was created. The Hospital fell under the aegis of the North East Metropolitan Regional Hospital Board, grouped with Mile End Hospital, St George's-in-the-East Hospital, St Peter's Hospital, and the East End Maternity Hospital. Major Green and Dr Gordon were appointed to serve on its Hospital Management Committee. Eventually there were four divisions – district, area, regional, and at the top, the Ministry of Health.

The ability to make major decisions on capital expenditure passed out of the hands of Hospital managers and the powerful House Committees to these outside bodies, to which all such requests had to be submitted. Applications were frequently referred on from the first to one or more of the other bodies before a final decision was reached, and more often than not even where a proposal was eventually approved in principle, shortage of funds within the Health Service necessitated a delay.

The days of strong-minded, autocratic chairmen in the Viscount Knutsford mould who effectively controlled hospital house committees and hospital governors, and almost single-handedly decided what money should be spent, and on what, were over. Speedy decisions became, of necessity, a thing of the past. In the twenty years from 1919, the managers of the London Jewish Hospital had, relying largely on their ability to raise the necessary funds from the Jewish community, completed the Hospital building, including medical and surgical wards, a separate children's ward, and operating theatres; created a large outpatient department; provided full kosher facilities and, in 1939, opened an up-to-date Nurses' Home. By comparison, it took ten years of persistent applications following nationalisation simply to improve the mortuary.

Administrative changes introduced over the years by successive governments inevitably generated periods during which all progress was halted. Looming general elections and the possibility of a change of government also had a delaying effect. Outgoing administrative bodies frequently stopped making decisions long before their demise, leaving responsibility for making them to their successors, and the new administrations then took time after entering office to reconsider the situation before taking the next step forward.

Despite their loss of effective power, the members of the former London Jewish Hospital Council of Management decided they still had a role to fulfil. They saw it as their duty to help preserve the Jewish atmosphere in the hospital by visiting patients, by checking that Jewish dietary laws were observed, and by advising on matters affecting other religious requirements, such as facilities for prayers, festivals and fasts. They continued to encourage the enlistment of Jewish staff, and determined to represent Jewish communal interests in any way possible. To assist them in these endeavours, and to help provide amenities not available through the National Health Service, they encouraged the formation of a League of Friends of the London Jewish Hospital that over the years to come gave them significant and substantial support. It was formally constituted in 1948 and began work the following year. The Friends arranged Purim tea parties for patients, and dances for the nurses and their friends. A trolley shop was taken round the wards each week. Mrs Ewan Montagu was its chairman for many years. Waverly Manor, the Maurice and Samuel Lyon House at 160 Great North Way, was maintained as a short stay home primarily for patients from the London Jewish Hospital. It is now a residential home administered by Jewish Care.

On nationalisation, certain assets remained as 'free monies' that individual hospitals might, with permission, have access to in special circumstances. Further, monies subscribed to voluntary hospitals between November 1946 and April 1948 could be used by the hospitals for capital expenditure of their own choice. The London Jewish Hospital raised sufficient during this period to enable them to build, equip and maintain a synagogue within the building, so that their hands would be strengthened in retaining the essentially Jewish environment of the hospital.

The Synagogue, designed by the architect Ernst Freud, was consecrated in October 1957. The Chief Rabbi, Israel Brodie, conducted the service assisted by Rev M. Zeffert, the Honorary Chaplain of the Hospital. Ernest Alexander, a member of the Hospital's original house committee, performed the official opening. Brodie said he was sure that the atmosphere that pervaded the Synagogue would give the worshippers a feeling of tranquillity.

'An Orphan Left on Their Doorstep by The Health Act'

The National Health Service has never had sufficient funds for all its needs. Priorities had to be established, and those of the small hospitals were low on the list. In a report made by the Manchester Jewish Hospital to the Board of Deputies in February 1951, the Hospital's Board of Management optimistically said that 'schemes involving capital expenditure, which previously would have been dependent upon special appeals, can now be initiated with reasonable prospects that approval will be given,' They, and the Managers of other small hospitals, were to learn that this was not to be.

Disillusionment soon set in. In a letter dated 22 February 1954[2] to Major F. M. Green, Chairman of the Hospital Council of Management, one of the Hospital's consultants, or possibly a member of the staff, (the available copy is unsigned), complained that the average members of the Area Management Committee were too remote from the detailed working of the hospitals they were managing.

The author said the Regional Board had no real interest in the London Jewish Hospital and was 'coldly indifferent' to its plans. The Board had shelved the Hospital's mortuary improvement proposal; its attitude to ritual circumcision was openly unsympathetic; and in its recent regional review it had dismissed the Hospital in a few words.

Clearly the Hospital does not fit with their scheme of things. They visualise it is an orphan left on their doorstep by the Health Act … It is idle to expect any help for any major capital improvements. It is with growing concern therefore, that I have watched at the Hospital Management Committee the gradual emergence of a policy of financial stringency towards the London Jewish Hospital.

The authorities suggested that a new Operating Theatre lamp should be paid for by the Friends, an item obviously an Exchequer liability, and the Regional Board even suggested that an urgently needed new operating theatre should be paid for by the Friends. The Regional Board then cut its amenity funding to the Hospital on the grounds that it received financial help from the League of Friends. This quite properly led to a protest that the Friends of the London Jewish Hospital were thereby subsidising hospitals without a Friends' Committee.

The nearby St George's-in-the-East Hospital was closed in 1956, leading to a loss of 200 beds in the Stepney district. This should have led to a greater demand on the space available at the London Jewish Hospital, but in fact the number of in-patients treated continued to fall. The Hospital had fewer patients in 1958 than it did in 1954. It was becoming clear that although there were vacant beds at the Hospital many Jewish patients preferred to go to hospitals nearer their homes, even though these made no religious provisions. In 1959 the Area Management Team sought the comments of the London Jewish Hospital Medical Committee on this. 'Why', they asked, 'are Jews going to other local hospitals, and why are general practitioners not referring their patients to the London Jewish Hospital despite the fact that there is a preponderance of Jewish general practitioners in the area?' They further expressed the opinion that unless urgent steps were taken the London Jewish Hospital would, within the next few years, either cease to exist or became a hospital for chronic cases only. This, a little more than ten years after the National Health Service was introduced, was the first official indication that closure of the London Jewish Hospital was a possibility.

The Medical Committee replied that the figures simply reflected the falling Jewish percentage of local population, and strongly contended that the main reason for the admittedly inadequate usage was the low structural and functional standard to which the Hospital had fallen and which the Health Authorities had failed to bring up to date. Despite their urgent requests for improvement to operating theatre facilities, for the provision of cubicles or side wards, for essential alterations to the paediatric ward and X-Ray department, little or nothing was done. The Medical Committee said they had little doubt that if the Area Management Team and the Regional Board would accept and implement the London Jewish Hospital Medical Committee's suggestions in full, the problems would vanish and the Hospital would meet the purpose for which it was established, and which it had understood would be maintained by the National Health Service. They said that if the Hospital were improved to the suggested standard, which was no more than the standards of any efficient hospital of like size, they were certain that they would regain the support of the general practitioners, and London's Jewish community would avail itself of the Hospital's services in greater numbers.

To the great disappointment of Drs. Gainsborough, Gordon, Klein, Prieskel, and Radcliffe, nothing whatsoever resulted from these representations. Their suggestions and views were either disregarded or dismissed by the Area Management Team.

The Nursing Staff

There was a further matter of serious concern. The London Jewish Hospital Medical Committee highlighted the general unhappiness of the nursing staff, a matter of complaint over a lengthy period. The Committee said that ever since the foundation of the Hospital there had been an inherent obligation to provide full nursing training for Jewish girls, a duty they were obliged to continue. It was the only hospital in London in which Jewish girls were able to achieve state registration in a strictly sectarian atmosphere. Now there was a serious shortage of nurses, and the fact that the Hospital managed to continue to function as well as it did was largely due to the devoted and invaluable service of those who remained.

In June 1950 the situation was described as 'bordering on the catastrophic', and the quality of the nurses has been described by a nurse who was there at the time as 'mixed'. Matters did not improve, and seven years later Hugh Gainsborough was still expressing his concern to Major Green that the shortage had reached danger level. Responsibility for twenty-two beds was often being left to one junior nurse. Few nurses stayed on to become staff nurses after qualification, and several junior nurses resigned.

The Hospital had been recognised by the General Nursing Council as a complete training school since 1923. Before World War II, standards were high. Certain problems arose during the latter part of the 1930s, but shortages were overcome by the recruitment of German Jewish probationers. Post-1948, with the falling off of work and declining standards, recognition was put severely at risk. In September 1960, a meeting under the Chairmanship of Councillor J. Samuels was held to discuss future plans. Prieskel, Gordon, and Miss B. H. Fawkes, the Education Officer of the General Nursing Council, were present. Miss Fawkes warned that the General Nursing Council would require training hospitals to provide sufficient clinical experience to afford all the practical training needed to prepare a student nurse for the full responsibilities of a State Registered Nurse, and she doubted whether the London Jewish Hospital could meet the criteria. She said she thought the Area Hospital Management Committee ought to give very serious consideration to the possibility of the London Jewish Hospital being demoted to the status of a Pupil Assistant Nurse Training School.

There was a strong possibility that the number of girls desiring to train in a religious atmosphere would still further decline if such a change were made. Eventually a compromise was reached; the London Jewish Hospital retained its training status, but during their third year the nurses attended four nearby specialist hospitals, spending three months at each. As a result their training remained of a high order, and in the majority of cases the nurses continued to live at the Hospital, thereby maintaining continuity of study and social life.

In the post war years, as with so many hospitals, foreign girls had to be accepted to meet the nursing requirements of the patients – but many were unsuitable for training and this was reflected in poor examination results. Through O.S.E., an international Jewish health organisation, a source of recruitment was opened up in Morocco and Iran from which highly intelligent Jewish girls were sent for training at the London Jewish Hospital, many of whom, once trained, returned to their own countries to supply the nursing services which did not exist there. For some years, a regular supply of suitable young Jewish girls came, and made a major contribution to the Hospital's well-being.

Structural Improvements

The only major structural improvements of any note following nationalisation were the reconstruction of the out-patient department, and a widening of the narrow passageway at the side of the Hospital needed to accommodate the wider modern ambulances then in service. Neither improvement was funded by the National Health Service.

In October 1960, Stepney Group Management Committee wrote to the Wolfson Foundation about the urgent need to undertake this work, stating that the proper functioning of the Hospital depended upon it. The scheme had been approved by the Hospital Management Committee, the Regional Board, and the Ministry of Health, and normally such a building scheme would be the responsibility of the Regional Board. However, the Board had other urgent commitments and could give no financial support. The sum needed was £65,000, and the Board had agreed to allow £40,000 of the Hospital's free monies to be used for the purpose. The

Foundation was asked if it would make a donation towards the balance. The Chief Rabbi, Israel Brodie and Dr Hugh Gainsborough wrote in support of the application. The Foundation generously agreed to give £25,000. When the out-patient department was opened in 1962 a commemoration plaque acknowledging the gift was installed and unveiled by Sir Isaac Wolfson.

Two years later, the Stepney Group Management Committee again approached the Foundation about plans that had been drawn up for a substantial rebuilding and re-equipment that would cost £500,000. The Foundation replied that it did not feel that it could help on this occasion. Yet a further application, this time for £65,000, was made in November 1965 to extend the nurses' accommodation, and the Foundation agreed to make the grant. Neither the previous Conservative government nor the incumbent Labour government had any compunction about accepting private money for National Health Service hospitals.

The Stanmore Plan

In desperation at the lack of National Health funding for what the Hospital's Medical Committee deemed essential work, and because the Jewish population of the East End continued its numerical decline, consideration was given to the possi-bility of building a private Jewish hospital in north-west London where more than 70% of London's Jewry then lived. Those in favour of the scheme thought that if a private hospital was built in that area, and if the National Health Service agreed to contract to take up a certain number of beds in it, then with support from charitable institutions or individuals, a successful new hospital could be established.

It took several years for the plan to mature; eventually in March 1964 it was announced that an option on a seventy-five acre plot of land had been acquired in Stanmore. Alfred Woolf, vice-president of the United Synagogue, and chairman of the organising committee, said[3] that the proposed hospital would be a memorial for the six million Jews killed during World War II. He anticipated that the total cost would be £2m. There was no intention to harm the London Jewish Hospital, but it had to be recognised that the majority of the London Jewish Hospital's prospective patients had moved out of the East End.

However, the following week there was an article in the *Jewish Chronicle* by Dr Abraham Marcus on the problems such a hospital would face.[4] He estimated the cost not at £2m. but between £3½ and £4m, and pointed out that the Joint Palestine Appeal, then the most successful Anglo-Jewish fund-raising organisation, collected just £2m. per annum. He further forecast that the annual running deficit would be likely to run into several hundred thousand pounds.

Support for Dr Marcus's view was expressed in a letter of 10 April 1964 signed by a glittering array of leading Jewish doctors, D. N. Baron, professor of chemical pathology at the Royal Free Hospital; Samuel J. Cohen, consultant physician at the London Hospital; S. B. Dimson, consultant paediatrician at the London Jewish Hospital; Harold Ellis, professor of surgery at Westminster Medical School; and Isaac Sutton, consultant psychiatrist at Friern Hospital. They felt the money would be better spent on a hospital or hostel for the chronic sick.

Miss Kitty Fishberg of 8 Black Lion Yard also cast doubt on the scheme, though from a different viewpoint, in a letter to the *Jewish Chronicle*:[5]

Sir,

Concerning the proposed new Jewish hospital in Stanmore, I think the Jewish community should ask themselves whether a Jewish hospital is necessary there. As a representative of the Finchley Combined Aid Committee I know that at present the London Jewish Hospital is in dire distress. I toured the hospital recently and hardly know where to begin to tell you of the Dickensian conditions prevailing there. For example, the kitchen equipment is the same as that which was installed forty years ago, and the children's ward was sadly overcrowded with one tiny bathroom and a hip bath. This serves also as the sister's office, sterilising room, etc. There is only one lift which carries food and patients. A new lift was about to be installed, but was stopped short on the first floor due to lack of funds.

There is no recreation room for the staff, an amenity which is most essential for the hard working staff who must have somewhere to relax if they are to continue to do their work well.

Why do these conditions prevail? The same conditions could occur in twenty years time with the proposed new hospital. My committee is of the opinion that the money would be better spent on bringing the present London Jewish Hospital up to date.

I would like to see a reawakening of Jewish interest in the Hospital. Although it is state aided, the amount contributed is sufficient only for the barest necessities of its day to day running. The Finchley committee is prepared to sponsor an appeal in aid of the London Jewish Hospital, but before doing so we would welcome any comments as to why this appeal should not go forward.

Mrs Ewan Montagu, chairman of the Friends of the London Jewish Hospital, felt the description of conditions at the Hospital were distorted. She pointed out that the out-patient department had recently been entirely rebuilt, and the children's ward was being enlarged, and claimed that under the jurisdiction of the Stepney Group Hospital Management Committee the Hospital was undergoing constant improvements and redecoration. Services were relayed to the wards from the Hospital's beautiful synagogue; there was a television set in every ward; each patient had a wireless that provided a choice of programmes; and a trolley telephone service was available on each floor.

No substantial funding was forthcoming, and the Stanmore plan was dropped.

Atmosphere

The staff found themselves in a hospital that was being administered by a body that seemingly had little interest in its continuing welfare; a hospital that was struggling to maintain its services while being kept desperately short of essential funding. Despite all these problems, and to the great credit of its staff, the Hospital retained its pre-1948 Jewish atmosphere, and so far as the patients were concerned created happy surroundings in which they could recover.

Several nurses and doctors who worked at the Hospital kindly gave interviews to the author. Joy Lyons, who joined as a student nurse in 1969,[6] described the Hospital as unique, with its own special homely ambience, particularly on Friday evenings and Saturdays when the nurses lit candles in every ward, *cholas* were served, and there were services in the synagogue. Elsie Landau invariably brought a home made cheesecake to each session she attended. There was a daily visit by Rabbi Nathan Bergerman, the honorary chaplain from 1958–78, a gentle man with a dry sense of humour, and by his wife, who also organised the out-patient canteen.

Dr Joseph Jacob, who was house physician and house surgeon in 1956/7 thought the atmosphere was something very special. There were still many older patients who felt more comfortable confiding personal matters to a Jewish doctor to whom they would relate more easily. There were also some patients who spoke only Yiddish, (many of the signs in the Hospital were still in Yiddish), and the fact that he was Jewish, and a former Yeshiva student too, was a bonus for them. They opened up. It was also, he said, the only hospital he knew where patients actively and strenuously engaged themselves in trying to arrange a *shidduch* for the bachelor doctors.

Mrs Alice Collins, who joined in 1958, trained there, and eventually served as a sister, said it was a very relaxed hospital. 'Wonderful! wonderful!. The staff, however hard they worked, went into the wards with smiles on their faces and kept them there'. Both Dr Jacobs and Mrs Collins considered the consultants to be of a quality one would expect at a teaching hospital and attributed much of the Hospital's happy character to them. 'There was not a weak link among them, and they were not money-grabbers'.

The patients displayed a good sense of humour, and that prevailed throughout the hospital. Nurses, too, were friendly amongst themselves, and did not form cliques, and quite a few found husbands for themselves from among the medical staff. Good discipline was maintained without resort to petty regulations.

Lysbeth Hurstbourne was at the London Jewish Hospital from 1954–79, joining as a night sister after training at Adenbrooke in Cambridge and spending time as a staff nurse at Lawn Road, (now part of the Royal Free Hospital), at Haslemere General Hospital, and at Hampstead General. She feels that the fact that there were doctors and nurses who could speak, or at least understand Yiddish, made a significant contribution to the atmosphere, particularly as quite a few patients still preferred to speak Yiddish even if they could also speak English. They could certainly swear in Yiddish, and on one occasion a nurse who was interpreting for her said 'I thought I knew every swear word there was to know, but I did not know half the cursing the man opposite just used to you Sister'. As Matron, Miss Hurstbourne had a significant role to play in maintaining standards in the latter years of the Hospital's life.

Renee Goldsmith (1950–3) said it was a comfortable, happy hospital, and both patients and staff felt involved in promoting its excellence. Sylvia Wallis, (1956–8), described it as a satisfying place for nurses because they were given more responsible work to do than in most other hospitals. Suzanne Leigh (1957–60) who was born in Morocco, said the whole place was very relaxed, and the English-born and foreign nurses got on well with each other. She was frequently invited to the homes of Jewish families for the Jewish Festivals. Rhoda Hackman (1974–9) who worked as secretary to the Hospital Secretary, Mr Edward Somerville, and also helped the social worker, said 'You could feel the Jewishness even though most patients were non-Jewish and the nursing staff were mainly Chinese and Phillipinos. The clinical assistants and the consultants were Jewish, and there was a lot of Jewish input. The volunteers in the canteen were Jewish, the food was still strictly kosher, and the plaques dotted everywhere in the wards and at the head of the beds were a continual reminder of the Hospital's origin'.

Anita Bloomberg was a nurse at the Manchester Victoria Memorial Jewish Hospital (1945–9), and was at the London Jewish Hospital in 1953 for a year and then again for eighteen months from the beginning of 1957. She considered the London Jewish Hospital a very friendly hospital and 'more Jewish' than the Manchester Hospital where some of the nurses were nuns.

They all attributed a great deal of the contentment the patients felt to the 'Jewish atmosphere', the very words the Haham, seventy years earlier, had used to describe as the real, if not the only, reason for the establishment of a Jewish Hospital.

COUNTDOWN TO CLOSURE

Throughout the 1960s small hospitals faced increasingly severe problems. The pattern of medicine was changing radically and rapidly. Investigation and treatment were becoming more complex, and some of the newer techniques could be carried out only in special units that by their nature had to be in, or associated with, large general hospitals.

Hopes of retaining the London Jewish Hospital as an acute hospital faded, and the possibility that the Jewish Welfare Board (today called Jewish Care) might assume control of the Hospital was explored, but that too came to nothing. On 12 Oct 1972, Melvyn Carlowe, its Executive Director, informed Dr Gordon that the Board could not 'take over' the hospital; 'one has only to look at the annual problems that the Home and Hospital at Tottenham has to keep its head above water to realise this is a commitment that our resources would be totally unable to cope with'.

The Medical Committee regretfully concluded that the only future for the Hospital was as a specifically Jewish hospital for longer stay cases, especially geriatric cases. The following year, the inevitable was accepted. On 5 October 1973, at a meeting between representatives of the North East Metropolitan Regional Hospital Board, the League of Friends, and the Board of Deputies, the decision was reached in principle that the London Jewish Hospital should be converted to a geriatric hospital, serving the Jewish community living in Tower Hamlets and elsewhere in the Metropolis.

One vital question to be considered was whether the London Jewish Hospital was suitable for such use. The gravest doubt was cast upon this. Dr C. P. Silver, consultant geriatrician to the Mile End Hospital, pointed out that ideally a geriatric hospital should preferably be ground floor only and set in a garden. At the London Jewish Hospital there were no grounds in which patients could sit or stroll, and there was no corridor system that patients could walk along as the wards were all on upper floors and opened directly on to stairs and lifts. Further, in case of fire, the isolation of the wards made matters particularly difficult for elderly patients. The critics had a very strong case.

Nonetheless, a rearguard action, led by Gordon and Prieskel, aided by Nancy

Hurstbourne, was fought, and every effort made to stave off the final day. Sir Keith Joseph, a government minister, was persuaded to take a personal interest, and local Members of Parliament, Mr Ian Mikardo and Mr Peter Shore gave such assistance as they could, but the end was never in doubt.

In November 1974 a Jewish Liaison Committee, under the Presidency of Mrs James de Rothschild and the Chairmanship of Mrs R. N. Carvalho, on which eight organisations were represented, was formed to continue negotiations about the Hospital's future.[1] Miss Hannah Hyman, the secretary of the Friends of the London Jewish Hospital became secretary of the new committee. It expressed the hope that the Hospital would become an acute geriatric hospital with its own assessment unit, day hospital, and diagnostic facilities, with half the beds available for Jewish patients from outside Tower Hamlets. By this time less than ten per cent of the patients lived in the East End, and it was extremely unlikely that any greater percentage could be attracted. Statistics for the period 1969–74 showed the number of beds in use was down from 128 to 90; occupation levels down from 77% to 72%; in-patient cases down from 2627 to 1318; and outpatients' attendance from 23,048 to 12,528.[2]

If there had been any doubts that closure was inevitable, a speech made in July 1975 by Barbara Castle, the Secretary of State for Health, to the National Association of Health Authorities would have removed them. She described the financial prospects for the National Health Service for the next few years as gloomy. There was no realistic possibility that a hospital such as the London Jewish Hospital could survive for much longer.

The following month, an official recommendation was made that the London Jewish Hospital should be closed forthwith. Nevertheless, the Liaison Committee decided to take every possible step, including sending a delegation to the Minister, to avert closure, or at least to extract some compensation, if for no other reason than as a measure of respect for those who had struggled so hard to establish the Hospital. The District authorities expressed sympathy, but echoed the Minister's words – 'as you know the outlook for the Health Service is daily becoming more bleak'.

Gordon continued actively to defend the hospital's suitability for geriatric care, but his arguments were clearly unsound – perhaps his judgement was clouded by his undoubted love and devotion to the Hospital – and it seems his colleagues realised this. They began to consider other options. They argued that if the Hospital could not continue, they would like some special provision to be made elsewhere for Jewish patients, and that this should be the *quid pro quo* for surrendering the London Jewish Hospital. They wanted the Hospital's Free Funds to be returned to the community, together with the proceeds of the sale of the site, although the latter was never a realistic objective.

F. M. Cumberlege, the Chairman of the City and East London Area Health Authority, said[3] that in the then strained financial situation of the National Health Service he did not see how the Authority could 'keep on with this place which costs us £¾ million a year to run', thus reviving echoes of Viscount Knutsford's statement of nearly seventy years earlier that it was ridiculous to spend £¼ million on a hospital for a few Jews who could not be bothered to learn the English language. Cumberlege and the District Management Team wanted the London Jewish Hospital to cease operating as soon as possible so that its running costs could be devoted to developments urgently needed elsewhere in the district.

One suggestion that emerged was that there should be a Jewish geriatric ward in one of the local hospitals, possibly the London Hospital, where orthodox Jews could enjoy their own customs and kosher food. If accepted, it would have entailed reversion to what had existed at the London Hospital during the nineteenth century and early part of the twentieth century. This did not find favour with the Liaison Committee which pointed out that the National Health Service had taken over a fully equipped hospital with 130 beds. In return for this the Jewish community was being offered a ward of a dozen beds. The Liaison Committee pressed for a feasibility study to be made to investigate whether there was any alternative to closure, and they persuaded the London Hospital and the District Management Team for Tower Hamlets to approach the chairman of the Regional Health Authority on this.

Meetings between the representatives of the Liaison Committee, the Board of Deputies, the local Members of Parliament, and the health authorities were leading nowhere. Cumberlege was in the unenviable situation of being attacked by both sides. The health authorities were insistent that the Hospital should be closed. They were exceeding the spending limits imposed by the government, and there was little or no prospect of capital monies being available in the next five years. The Regional Board was exerting pressure on the Area Health Authorities to reduce costs. Further, the then current view in National Health Service circles was that geriatric beds and services should be within the easiest possible reach of relatives and friends, and should be erected within general hospitals in order to achieve the best possible access to diagnosis and therapeutic and rehabilitative services.

Nothing concrete emerged from the numerous discussions, representations, and the collection of signatures on protest petitions, and in April 1976 the formal consultation process that could lead to closure was set in motion by the City and

East London Area Health Authority. The Authority favoured providing a Jewish ward in another hospital in the district for the use only of those elderly Jews who were living in Tower Hamlets; the Liaison Committee wanted the existing buildings to be adapted to care for Jewish and non-Jewish patients together, the Jewish patients being drawn from any part of London.

The Liaison Committee put out a statement:[4]

We emphatically confirm that the Jewish community, of which it is the representative, would deeply resent it and would regard it as a most serious breach of faith, if the Hospital were closed without fully satisfactory alternative provisions being made and if the Hospital and its site (which were purchased and erected by voluntary contributions from the Community) were sold and the proceeds used for other purposes ... In 1948 the Hospital did not exercise its right to opt out of the National Health Service. Had it been thought at that time that there would ever be the slightest possibility of the community losing its Hospital, there can be no doubt whatsoever that the Hospital would have remained outside the National Health Service.

In the light of what is now known, this was a doubtful argument. The London Jewish Hospital had been in no position in 1948 to opt out of the Health Service.

Palliative replies were given to the Liaison Committee to the effect that the health authorities had been deeply impressed by the sincerity and strength of purpose shown by the representatives of the Hospital and the Jewish community, and said that if money were no problem the authorities would have suggested a new building complex for Jewish geriatric patients from any area of residence; but, it was hastily added, there was scant prospect of obtaining enough capital to meet the needs of the local community, let alone a community further afield. It was estimated that there were by now only 8,000 Jews resident in the East End compared with 100,000 or more at the start of the century. At this stage of the negotiations it was simply a question of how long the delay would be, and what financial recompense could be extracted.

The Liaison Committee applied sufficient pressure for Roland Moyle, the Minister of State for Health, to decide to visit the Hospital. There he was met by Dr Gordon, Miss Hurstbourne, and Mrs A. Collins. He was also introduced to the Catering Officer, Mrs L. Nasseen, Sister Mrs W. Balasunderam, and the Superintendant Physiotherapist Mrs R. Gurari whose names are indicative of the changes the Hospital had undergone. On the day of this visit,[5] Gordon was interviewed on Capitol Radio and said it would be a wicked shame to close a hospital that was in excellent condition and could provide a first class service for elderly Jewish sick.

The Committee's forceful representations had some effect. The Minister told

Mikardo that he had asked the Regional Health Authority to reconsider its decision. This effectively meant the Minister was avoiding making a decision on the merits of the case and passing the buck back to the Region which would have to have further consultations with the Area Health Authority.

Cumberlege reacted to this delaying tactic by asking Moyle to give his consent to the temporary closure of the Hospital pending his final decision. Moyle rejected the suggestion, and pointed out that the Central Council for Jewish Social Services was concerned that in addition to the London Jewish Hospital, the Bearsted Memorial Hospital was also under threat (it was subsequently closed). Reading between the lines, his letter to Cumberlege made it clear that though officially the decision had not been made, when it was made it would be a decision for closure.

The Authorities put further pressure on the Minister to sign the closure notice.[6] It was pointed out that it was over two years since the Area Authority had opened formal consultations, and a year and four months since the Minister was asked by the Liaison Committee and the London Borough of Tower Hamlets to make a quick decision. But the then Secretary of State for Health, David Ennals, decided to defer the decision until after the coming general election, an election that the Labour Party lost.

The incoming Conservative minister, Dr Gerard Vaughan, sought the advice of Sir Keith Joseph on the proposed closures of the London Jewish Hospital and the Bearsted Memorial Hospital. 'Have there as far as you know been any thoughts for a national private Jewish hospital?' he asked 'Alternatively, is there general support in your view for old people's homes for the Jewish community?.[7] Sir Keith consulted Melvyn Carlowe who wrote to him on 3 August 1979 informing him that the Board did not consider the London Jewish Hospital suitable for its Part III (residential accommodation) needs. On the question of a private national Jewish hospital, Carlowe said none of the communal organisations was in a position to fund this.

Dr Gordon, Donald Samuel, (a member of the Council of Friends and of the Liaison Committee and chairman of Waverley Manor), and A.M.Jacob, (Chairman of the London Jewish Hospital), met on 28 August 1979 and agreed that they would no longer seek to retain the Hospital within the National Health Service. They decided to concentrate their efforts on trying to raise sufficient monies to bring the Hospital and its site into the hands of the Jewish community, and if that failed then to try to persuade the Ministry to support the release of the Free Monies back to the community.

On 24 September 1979 the decision was made for the 'temporary' closure of the Hospital on the weekend of 27/28 October. This took place, and it fell to Rhoda Hackman to turn the key in the lock. The Hospital never reopened, despite threats of a strike-in by members of the National Union of Public Employees. Security measures were taken, and security guards patrolled the site at a cost of almost £1,000 a week.

The possibility of a purchase or a lease of the site by the Jewish community was then considered at length. The Friends eventually negotiated an option to purchase the site and its buildings for £460,000. They proposed to sell the Nurses' Home to a Housing Association, and adapt the main building as a Part III Home for about 110 severely infirm aged, with residential accommodation for nursing staff and excellent facilities for residents, staff and visitors. The Synagogue, 'of great artistic merit', and the kosher kitchens would be kept. They estimated that after making allowance for the proceeds of the sale of the Nurses' Home £900,000 was needed. They confidently anticipated receiving at least £200,000 from the Free Funds held by the Health Authorities, and the trustees of the Levy Family trusts were prepared to secure future income of approximately £5,000 p.a. Once again, an approach was made to the Wolfson Foundation.

However, when the Friends received a more detailed estmate from their architect, Mr Alex Flinder, this showed a provisional budget for the main hospital building alone of £1,178,000. When professional fees, value added tax, medical equipment, work to the Synagogue, work to the mortuary and other items were taken into account, the figure was nearer £1$\frac{1}{2}$m than £900,000.

On 27 January 1981, Alex Jacob informed the Minister that because of the economic climate, growing doubts as to the suitability of the location, and appeals for other major developments, the Committee had reluctantly concluded they could not raise sufficient money, and that they had to decline the offer to purchase the site.

The Minister was amenable to the transfer of the free monies, subject to the views of the Charity Commissioners being sought. Negotiations dragged on for a further four years. The Friends had the opportunity to purchase two houses adjoining Waverley Manor, and wanted to use the funds for this purpose. Eventually, on 31 July 1985, there was a meeting at the offices of the Charity Commissioners at which representatives of Tower Hamlets Health Authority, the City and Hackney Health Authority, and the Friends were present. There was general agreement that 5% of the available funds should go to City and Hackney. There was deadlock over the remaining 95%. Jacobs contended that the Friends should receive 80%, Tower Hamlets representatives urged that the Friends should receive only 65%. The recommendation of the Charity Commissioners to the Minister was that the Friends should receive 70%, a total of £313,291, and this was accepted by all the parties.

The saga had reached its end.

CONCLUSIONS

How far did the various arguments raised during the debate prove to be correct? The language problem was probably exaggerated, and it is more likely that those who claimed that there was always someone on hand at the general hospitals to translate, were right. Doctors quickly found a way of identifying symptoms from patients who could not speak English. The existence of the Hospital did not greatly reduce the number of poor Jews who attended the medical missions, nor lead to their closure – they closed only after most East End Jews had left the area.

Once established, the rich did not, as the Haham feared, displace those who had struggled to open the Hospital. Instead they took up the role of generous supporters, as Berliner had forecast they would, particularly the Rothschilds and Bernhard Baron. And far from causing anti-Semitism and lowering Jews in the estimation of their neighbours, the existence of the London Jewish Hospital provoked admiration, and non-Jews sought its services in ever increasing numbers until, indeed, they were the majority. Further, the wealthy section of the Jewish community continued their generous support for the older hospitals.

Yet the Hospital, eventually successful, had a disappointing end. The highest hopes of its founders were never fully realised. There was undoubtedly a serious decline in its standards following nationalisation due to the chronic lack of funding, exacerbated by the fact that its consultants were getting older and not being replaced.

The Hospital paid the price for being out of time. It was struggling to open when immigration was falling and voluntary hospitals had started upon their terminal decline. Post-1945, small hospitals were out of fashion, and the Jewish East End population had dwindled to less than 10,000. The difference in the quality of service it could provide compared to other general hospitals gradually widened, and from the 1950s onwards it had to refer more and more of its complicated cases to the London Hospital. Berliner and his friends achieved a moral victory, but a strategic failure. They had not forseen, perhaps could not have forseen, the developments that were to occur.

The Manchester Victoria Memorial Jewish Hospital followed a very similar path. Progress was followed by decline after 1948, and for similar reasons. By

1908 it had forty beds, eventually increased to just over one hundred. Winston Churchill, who was made a Life Governor for his contributions to the Hospital, officially opened the out-patient department in 1908. With difficulty, it overcame a financial crisis in 1914. In 1922, Nathan Laski, originally an opponent, was appointed Chairman of the Board of Management and continued in that office until his untimely death in a car accident in 1941. He was succeeded by his son Neville. The Earl of Derby opened a new Nurses' Home in 1926, and in 1927 the Hospital was recognised as a Training School by the Royal College of Nursing.

In 1930, the Hospital was the second in the country to adopt the system of awakening patients at 7 a.m. instead of 5.30 a.m. From 1932 it operated a private wing; beds in a two-bed room were available at £4.4.0 per week, and single rooms at prices not exceeding £7.7.0 per week. 'All rooms are beautifully furnished and fitted, complete with hot and cold water. These prices are inclusive of X-ray, massage etc. and there are no extra charges. Surgeons' and Physicians' fees are adjusted to meet the needs of each case'. A Bernhard Baron Wing was opened in 1933.

In December 1940 the Hospital was hit by enemy bombs; five members of staff were killed and the Nurses' Home was destroyed. A new Nurses' Home was opened in 1954 and a new out-patient department in 1961. The Hospital gradually wound its services down, and finally closed its wards in 1988, and its out-patient department in November 1990.

The struggle to establish Jewish Hospitals in London and Manchester highlighted the different attitudes, needs, and desires of the established community and the new arrivals; of the rich and the poor. By provoking a public debate it eventually, to some extent, brought the two sides closer to each other. The rich bowed to the sustained pressure, although not until it was inevitable that they should do so. Then, as had happened so often before in the Jewish community, they accepted the situation, supplied the essential continuing finance, and sought to gain a measure of control over the institutions. But in the case of the Manchester and London Jewish hospitals the end result was somewhat different from the usual. The participation of the rich was not entirely on their own terms. Those who had engaged in the long and difficult struggle accepted the belated assistance, gratefully and graciously, but they heeded the warning of the Haham. No oligarchy was established; the enthusiasm of the poorer subscribers remained undiminished. Although a Rothschild became titular head at the London Jewish Hospital, and indeed worked assiduously for the Hospital, the administration, organisation and major control remained with those who had fought so hard to establish it.

Today, a new, modern, up-to-date Jewish Hospital, even if thought desirable, would be unrealisable. The declining Jewish population, probably no more than 283,000 in Britain, and less than 197,000 in Greater London,[1] could not sustain it. Language is no longer a problem,[2] and the National Health Service has had considerable experience in caring for Jewish patients. Most hospitals are aware of the need for early burial, and kosher food can be purchased from commercial suppliers.

It is now widely acknowledged within the Health Service that an inability of health workers to communicate with ethnic minority patients, or an unawareness of particular cultural practices which might affect the acceptability of health advice, can result in poorer quality services, or no services at all, to this segment of the community, Some health authorities provide their staff with practical guidelines covering a range of sensitive issues for minority patients, including guides to cultural customs. Interpreters are more freely available, some being employed on a sessional or full-time basis. It is also recognised that racist attitudes may cause individual workers to deny services to ethnic minorities, to treat them with less care, and this is a problem that is being addressed.

The pioneers who struggled to establish the London Jewish Hospital would have been saddened by post-World War II events. Many of them might have welcomed the National Health Service, but they would have been dismayed by the sad decline in the Hospital's standards.

Nothing can detract from the achievement of the Jewish East End working classes in establishing the Hospital. For sixty years it stood as a proud symbol of the ability of many little people to achieve a very large goal through single-minded determination against almost overwhelming odds. The Hospital was a proud testament to their abilities, and fulfilled an important service to the wider community as well as to the Jews for whom it was originally intended.

Fierce pride still exists among the descendants, not only of Berliner and his family and of those who held office in the Association, but also of those whose fathers or grandfathers bought a square foot of land, or a brick, or went round with a collecting box, and then passed on the memory of the struggle to the younger generation. At another time, or perhaps if he had lived a little longer, Berliner would have probably been awarded a state honour.

The Hospital undoubtedly provided a much desired addition to the tally of hospital beds for the inhabitants of the East End, but if only it had been established fifty years or more earlier, it would have been open and would have flourished when it was, without question, most needed. It would have been a particular boon for the first generation of poor Jews who flooded into the East End from Eastern

Europe from 1880 onwards, and much unnecessary distress would have been avoided.

An independent hospital now stands on the original site. Its initial cost was £18m.

THE INTRODUCTION OF THE NATIONAL HEALTH SERVICE

[1] Only the teaching hospitals kept their endowments.

[2] Only an unsigned copy of this letter is available. Its contents indicate that its author was one of the hospital's consultants.

[3] *Jewish Chronicle*, 13 March 1964.

[4] 20 March 1964.

[5] 27 March 1964.

[6] Her third year of training was spent at the Salvation Army Mothers' Home, Clapham; St Clements'; Moorfields; and Great Portland Street Hospital.

COUNTDOWN TO CLOSURE

[1] The constituent bodies were the Board of Deputies; Friends of the London Jewish Hospital; the Jewish Home and Hospital at Tottenham; the Home for Aged Jews (Nightingale House); the Jewish Welfare Board; the League of Jewish Women; the Maurice and Samuel Lyon Home (Waverley Manor); and Stepney Jewish (B'Nai Brith) Clubs and Settlement.

[2] The general population of Tower Hamlets was also declining. It fell by 15% between 1971 and 1981.

[3] In a letter dated 28 August 1975 to D. J. Kenny, the District Administrator of the Tower Hamlets Health District.

[4] 13 October 1975.

[5] 18 February 1977.

[6] Letter 1 June 1978 from District Adminstrator to the Minister.

[7] Letter of 19 July 1979.

CONCLUSIONS

[1] Figures supplied in November 1999 by Marlena Schmool, Executive Director of the Community Research Unit of the Board of Deputies.

[2] Yiddish is still spoken widely among certain orthodox groups, particularly in the Stamford Hill area of London, but they also speak English.

GLOSSARY

Ashkenazim, Jews of Central and Eastern European origin

Brith Melah, Circumcision ceremony

Chanukah, Festival of Lights, usually occurring in December

Cheder/chederim, Traditionally a small room in a teacher's home in which young boys are educated

Chola, A braided loaf of soft sweet bread glazed with egg white

Chutspah, Hard to believe effrontery; brazenness; shamelessness

Esrog and Lulav, Citron and palm leaf for ceremonial use in the Festival of Tabernacles

Goyim, Non-Jews

Haham, Chief Rabbi of the Sephardi community

Heim, The Homeland; the Old Country

Heimische, Homely

Meshugga, Crazy; obsessed

Mezzuzah, Case enclosing religious verses written on a parchment scroll and affixed to the doorframes of a house

Mitzvah, A kind deed; an ethical act

Mohel, A person licensed to perform circumcision

Purim, The Feast of Esther

Rachmonas, Genuinely felt pity and sympathy

Rebbetzan, Rabbi's wife

Schnorrer, Beggar or scrounger

Sephardi, Jews of Spanish, Portuguese, and Middle Eastern origin

Shidduch, An arranged marriage

Shofar, Ram's horn used as trumpet in Jewish ceremonies

Shtetl, East European village or small town

Simchot Torah, Festival of the Rejoicing of the Law

Stieble, Small, informal synagogue; often just a room in a house

Talmud Torah, A school in which the Torah and other religious subjects are studied

Tephillin, Phylacteries worn by Jewish men during morning prayers

Wacher, Person who attends to Jewish bodies after death and before burial

Yeshiva, A Jewish college of learning

SELECT BIBLIOGRAPHY

Abel-Smith, B., *The Hospitals 1800–1948* (1964)
  A history of the nursing profession (1960)
Bermant, Chaim, *The Cousinhood* (1971)
Black, Gerry, *Health and Medical Care of the Jewish Poor in the East End of London 1880–1914*. Unpublished Ph.D. thesis. Leicester. (1987)
  Living Up West. Jewish Life in London's West End (1994)
  J.F.S. The History of the Jews' Free School, London since 1732 (1998)
Black, Eugene C., *The Social Politics of Anglo-Jewry 1880–1920* (1988)
Bloom, Cecil, *Jewish Dispersion Within Britain* in *Patterns of Migration 1850–1914*, Newman A. and Massil S. (Eds)
Burke, Thomas, *The Real East End* (1932)
Cameron, H. C., *Mr. Guy's Hospital 1726–1948* (1954)
Cesarani, David, *The Jewish Chronicle and Anglo-Jewry 1841–1991* (1994)
Clark-Kennedy A. E., *The London. A Study in the voluntary hospital system* (1962)
  London Pride (1979)
Courtney, Dainton, *The Story of England's Hospitals* (1961)
Dutt, G. C., *Health care for Bangladeshis Abroad* (1995)
Encyclopaedia Britannica 11th edition 1911
Englander, David, *A documentary history of Jewish immigrants in Britain 1840–1920* (1994)
Finestein, Israel, *Jewish Society in Victorian England* (1993)
Fishman, William J. *East End Jewish Radicals 1875–1914* (1975)
Gainer, Bernard, *The Alien Invasion. Origins of the Aliens Act 1905* (1972)
Garrard, John A., *The English and Immigration. A comparative study of Jewish Influx 1880–1910* (1971)
Gartner, Lloyd, *The Jewish Immigrant in England – 1870–1914* (1960)
Gidney, W. T., *History of the London Society for Promoting Christianity Amongst The Jews 1809–1908* (1908)
Henriques, Basil L., *The Indiscretions of a Warden* (1937)
Hodgkinson, Ruth G., *The Origins of the National Health Service* (1967)
Holmes, Colin, *Anti-Semitism in British Society 1876–1939*. New York (1979)
Hymanson, Albert, *The Sephardim of England* (1951)
Jacobs, Joseph, *Studies in Jewish statistics* (1891)

Jewish Chronicle, *The Jewish Chronicle 1841–1941. A century of newspaper History* (1949)

Knutsford, Viscount, *In Black and White. An autobiography* (1926)

Langton, Neville, *Prince of Beggars. A biography of Lord Knutsford* (1923)

Lipman Vivian, *Social History of the Jews in England 1850–1950* (1954)
A Century of Social Service 1859–1959. The History of the Jewish Board of Guardians (1959)

Marks, Lara, *'Dear Old Mother Levy's'. The Jewish Maternity Home and Sick Room Helps Society 1895–1939* (1990). The Society for the Social History of Medicine

Melnick, Samuel C., *Giant among Giants* (1994)

Morris, E. W., *A History of the London Hospital* (1926)

Newman, Aubrey (Ed), *Provincial Jewry in Victorian Britain* (1975)

Newman, Aubrey, *The United Synagogue 1870–1970* (1977)

Owen, David, *English Philanthropy 1660–1960*. Cambridge Mass. (1964)

Pollins, Harold, *Hopeful travellers; Jewish Migrants and Settlers in Nineteenth Century Britain*. Leicester (1986)
Economic History of the Jews in England (1982)

Poynter, F. N. L. (Ed), *The evolution of hospitals in Britain* (1964)

Procheska, F. L., *Philanthropy and the Hospitals. The King's Fund 1897–1990* (1992)

Rivett, Geoffrey, *The development of the London Hospital System 1823–1982* (1986)

Roth, Cecil, *History of the Great Synagogue London 1690–1940* (1950)

Rubinstein, W. D. *A History of the Jews in the English-Speaking World: Great Britain* (1996)

Russell C. and Lewis H. S., *The Jew in London* (1900)

Walker, Henry, *East London* (1896)

INDEX